Grand
Distance

SUSAN HOFFMAN

Grand Distance

Nothing Could Stop Her from Seeing her Grandson Grow Up

SUSAN HOFFMAN

Cover photo: Richard Ortega
Author photo and front cover: Mandi Blanton
Interior layout: BeaPurplePenguin.com

Collegare Press

If not for the love of Jacob, I would
not have traveled down the unlikely
path where I would meet all of you.

This book is for all
of the grandparents.

Introduction

What would you do if you were forbidden
to see your grandchild?

Would you curl up in ball and want to die?

Would you wait until the child turned eighteen?

Would you go to court and fight?

Would you beg and plead for mercy?

Would you offer a financial incentive?

Would you try to change the law?

or

Would you break the rules?

CHAPTER 1

The Feeling

TO A GRANDPARENT, not being able to see a grandchild feels like living with a wound that never heals.

Working with disenfranchised grandparents over the years I have witnessed just about every reaction and response. I have also experienced them. There is no order to the way grandparents deal with separation from a grandchild, the common thread being, overwhelming grief and sadness.

Some grandparents become depressed to the point they want to roll up in a ball and die. The deep sorrow can become paralyzing, and long lasting for some.

Others jump into fight mode where they land in court suing for grandparent visitation.

Some continue to plead and beg for forgiveness looking for ways to make amends for whatever they did or (didn't do) to cause the alienation.

Some pay money to see their grandkids.

Some think they can change the law and that will solve the problem and get them visitation.

Finally, there are the rule breakers—a handful who go rogue and seek alternative ways to see the grandkids—from a distance.

Relationships take many forms and sometimes we have to come up with innovative ways to continue a relationship with a loved one. Just because we can no longer be in someone's life physically, doesn't mean the relationship is over, it's just different. And once a bond has developed, it lasts forever. That was the case in my situation. My grandson and I developed a loving bond during the first five years of his life and when I was told by his mother and adoptive father that I could no longer see him, I hatched what could be described as an unorthodox plan of action.

CHAPTER 2

The Bond

I DIDN'T EXPECT to feel such instant love wash over me the minute Jacob's mother told me of his birth. Three days later I arrived at the apartment in Orange where they lived.

None of it had seemed real until the phone call, when I felt the jolt of emotions bubbling inside me, and that's when it hit me that he was part of me and I was now a grandmother and connected to this little human being.

My son and Jacob's mother went their separate ways. They were young and he wasn't ready to start a family. Even though my son wasn't involved with his child. I on the other hand, was.

The mom and I developed a friendly relationship that was centered around Jacob. I made sure that she knew that I would always be there for her and Jacob one hundred percent.

I owned a children's clothing store on Balboa Island which was an economical benefit and a gratifying experience for me to be able to outfit the baby.

Jacob's mother would bring him into the store and we would sit on the floor with piles of outfits to sort through. We dressed and undressed him in new outfits sort of like playing dolls.

Baby's first Christmas was celebrated in early January, when my teen daughter and I delivered gifts to his home. It was so much fun to see him growing so fast and be so alert as he played with the bows and wrapping paper.

When Jacob was seven months old, I became his babysitter one night a week while his mom took classes to earn her college degree so she could someday become a teacher.

Every Monday night, I would leave work at four in the afternoon so I could be in Orange in time for her to get to her 5:30 night class.

I fed and bathed him, changed his diapers, played with him and rocked him until he fell asleep in my arms. Once I wrote in his photo album, "I can't believe how big your eyes are. You look so peaceful, so beautiful sleeping in my arms. I don't want to let you go and put you in your bed."

On a Sunday in March of the same year, I was asked to watch the now eight month old Jacob so that his mom could have a day to spend with her friends. Jacob's mom was enjoying food and drinks at a big table with a group of friends at a Fashion Island eatery, when I arrived around noon. He fussed at first as I took him away from the action, but once we got in the car he settled down. Since I didn't have a carseat, we transferred Jacob's carseat and stroller from his mother's car to mine and off we went to Grandma's house.

This was the first time that I had had him all to myself in my house. But when I tried to put him down for a nap, he wasn't having any of it. He won that battle and after twenty minutes of crying, I packed him in his stroller and took him for a long walk from my house on Balboa Island to Corona del Mar State Beach.

His mom was having a good time and decided to leave him with me until after ten o'clock that night, which was the longest length of time that I had taken care of him. Fortunately I had previously set up the maple crib that had been stored in the attic for many years and now it was all decked out with brand new blue and white gingham bedding and stuffed animals in anticipation of many future sleepovers. The visit ended up becoming significant, since it would be the only time that Jacob would ever sleep in the crib that had once been his father's.

Although I looked forward to the weekly babysitting, sometimes the apartment felt claustrophobic, and that's when I'd take baby Jacob outside for walks around the neighborhood. We would go to the small pocket park down the street or to the nearby grocery store before it got dark. Then I would climb the steep open stairway with baby in one arm and the stroller in the other.

To give Jacob a change of scenery I sometimes packed him in my car along with his stroller and took him to my house for a couple of hours. It didn't matter that I had literally just come from that direction and now I was turning around and going back to where I had just come from. The Balboa Island trips did him good though, he got to experience new sights and sounds.

13

On one of our strolls, we stopped to visit with my friend John, who had been sitting in a weathered Adirondack chair on his front porch. As we were about to leave, he raised his index finger and said, "Wait here a sec, I have an idea." He dashed inside and returned in a flash with a bag of breadcrumbs in hand.

I removed Jacob from his stroller and we followed John onto the beach that was in front of his house. The three of us sat on the seawall with Jacob perched on my lap as John tossed the bread pieces into the air and toward the ducks swimming near the water's edge of the bay. Soon we were surrounded by hungry, quacking ducks begging for more food.

Jacob was mesmerized by the commotion and when John paused for a moment, he pressed his little hand on John's arm as a way of asking him to continue. Startled, John whipped his head around to see what I wanted, and when I told him that Jacob had been the one to tap his arm, he didn't believe that a ten-month old baby could do such a thing.

Jacob's first birthday was coming up in July and when I inquired about celebration plans to his mom, she explained that she was having a party, and no, I wouldn't be invited. It would be awkward with all of her family there and make everyone uncomfortable if I was there. That was a head scratcher for sure. What was I supposed to say? Not wanting to make an issue, I managed an "Ok, I understand." But it wasn't ok, and I didn't understand. My feelings were hurt being treated like an outsider.

Jacob didn't know the difference, so we made alternate plans for another day to celebrate. I took baby and Mom out to lunch at a restaurant close to their apartment where he opened his gifts as he sat in the high chair.

Just before Christmas, Jacob's mother brought him to my house for a visit, which would be our Christmas celebration. The three of us walked to nearby Wilma's Patio and then we took Jacob to watch the holiday boat parade along the Balboa Island bay front. At seventeen months old, he seemed to enjoy the excitement of the lights and music and people milling around.

With the new year came an end to my regular babysitting job when his mom's school schedule changed and Jacob was enrolled in day care. I no longer saw him weekly but I made a point to visit at least once a month and whenever it was convenient for his mother. She had a busy schedule with school and work and I worked six days a week running my store, but I managed to visit if only for a short time. I understood that with a baby establishing a consistent presence early on is vital to creating a bond.

CHAPTER 3

The New Normal

MY VISITS WITH Jacob had been consistent since his birth, but that all changed when my son came back into the picture. He filed a petition for visitation after he was denied visits by Jacob's mother, which also changed the status quo between she and I.

What I didn't count on was her wrath toward me for supporting my son and helping him retain legal counsel. Once attorneys got involved the animosity only got worse. Although Jacob's mother had asked me about my son several times for the first year, now twenty months later she said that it was too late and she didn't want my son involved. I guess I had thought she would be happy that Jacob's dad was taking responsibility.

The first court appearance was a hearing that ended without resolution, which then led to a trial scheduled for two weeks later.

My son took the stand and admitted to the judge that he had screwed up but was now willing to take responsibility.

Jacob's mom countered with accusations to support her dissension. She testified that since he had been absent for two years that disqualified him as a fit parent and therefore should not be given visitation.

The general assumption being that access to both parents is in the best interest of a child, the judge ruled in favor of my son having court ordered visitation.

The judge came up with a step-up plan of monitored visits that gradually increased from two hour monitored visits to six hour unmonitored over the next three months.

Once court was adjourned and everyone was outside the courtroom, Jacob's mom lost her temper. Her mother tried to calm her down but she was ranting about the injustice of the decision. Both attorneys were in a huddle working out the logistics of the order with the tantrum escalating nearby. When my son's attorney approached me he lowered his voice as he leaned closer, saying, "you may want to think about filing for grandparent rights."

I stared at him as if he had been speaking a foreign language, and responded, "what's that?"

He said, "you file a petition in court requesting your own separate visitation."

I said, "oh no, she would never keep me away from Jacob."

He shook his head with a smirk on his face as he watched the tirade.

CHAPTER 4

The Visits

I WAS ON pins and needles waiting to hear how my son's first visit went. When the call finally came, his first words, through tears were, "Mom he looks just like me."

I let out a sigh of relief. "Tell me more, how did everyone get along?"

He described the visit as kind of icy at first then Jacob's mom warmed up and they ended up having a nice time. He said that Jacob was a cool kid and that he helped feed him a hot dog for lunch.

I was so happy I could hardly stand it and couldn't wait to be a part of it.

The visits were moving along, that is until it was time to take Jacob out of the house. Prior to that, all visits had been monitored by Mom. When we arrived, on Saturday, Mom had gone back to being sullen. We had planned on taking

Jacob to the park and McDonalds. He was eager to go with us and when I placed him in the borrowed car seat all hell broke loose. The seat wasn't stable enough because there was some movement and after fooling with it for 30 minutes, Mom said we couldn't go because the seat wasn't right. "You have an old car and the carseat won't work," was her explanation.

I asked if we could borrow her car seat, since that's what I had used during the two years that I drove Jacob.

She refused.

The saddest part of this ordeal was Jacob's disappointment. He was buckled in with a smile of anticipation on his face, ready to go.

There would be no McDonalds.

I even asked if she wanted to go? She didn't.

My son was beside himself, with his short fuse, he threw up his hands in frustration and walked away. Mom followed him and gave him a piece of her mind. He dropped a few F-bombs and the two of them went at it while Jacob watched from the backseat as the argument escalated.

He argued that she was unreasonable. She argued that we should have had a better car seat. I suggested that we make the most of it and take Jacob for a walk to the small park that was part of the apartment complex?

By the time we got to the park, my son was still fuming. In the mean time, the mom had called her parents and now it truly was a three ring circus which began over a car seat. Which really wasn't what this was about. It all had to do with control and fear of losing her property (Jacob) once he was out of sight.

My next idea was to go and buy a new car seat and try to

save what was left of our visit that included a trip to McDonalds. Thirty minutes later, I returned with a brand new Eddie Bauer car seat from a nearby Target. Everyone seemed to have calmed down by then, well everyone except maybe Jacob who was now playing alone in the plastic sandbox on his patio. I did everything I could to coax him into going for a ride, but all I got was a head shake and a "no." Kids know when things aren't right.

The last visit in the step-up program took place in December. This was a big one because I wanted a holiday family photo featuring five generations, a rare event that not many people can experience. My son, daughter and I arrived promptly at 10 a.m. to pick up Jacob. We were allotted two hours to take the photo, travel from Orange to Upland and back again. No exceptions even for a 101 year old. My grandmother was living in a nursing home in Upland and because of her age and health, there was no delaying the moment. My aunt and uncle got my grandma ready and wheeled her outside to the grassy area where my dad would join us for the photo. It had taken us 45 minutes to get there and with the clock ticking, we quickly assembled the five generations in chronological order on a picnic bench as my uncle hurriedly snapped several photos. This was the first time my grandma and aunt and uncle had seen Jacob and sadly there was no time to enjoy the moment. Even Jacob wanted to run and play with the big purple ball my dad brought for him, but after a few kicks we hustled him back into the car for the quick turnaround.

The drive back was like an "e" ticket ride the way my son was driving so we could get back in time. I sat in the back seat with Jacob as he nodded off. I felt bad that we hadn't stopped to feed him. It was hard to know what to do under the circumstances. We delivered Jacob back at 12:05, and got scolded for not feeding him lunch.

With the two hour visits now behind us, our first six hour visit would be on Christmas Day and I could hardly contain myself. We were headed out the door to pick up Jacob when the phone rang. We were told that he was sick and couldn't come over. My son hung up, shook his head, let loose with a few expletives and then plopped himself on the couch and flipped on the TV. Not giving up so easily, I called right back and asked if we could come over to their place with his gifts? Mom said, "No." Everyone in our family anticipating a visit with the grandchild was more than disappointed when they learned he wouldn't be there. It was a let down for all of us.

After that I had no interest in celebrating Christmas, in fact that was the last time that I had a tree. Christmas had been sucked out of my life like air from a deflated balloon; the celebratory moment was gone.

The next visit didn't happen because my son was thirty minutes late and Mom was gone by the time we arrived. I was required to meet my son at their apartment and then use my car to transport Jacob because my son had a truck with no back seat. He was driving two hours from San Diego as it was. It would have been much easier to simply let me pick up Jacob and meet him at my house on Balboa Island, easier yes, but nothing was easy when it came to navigating visits. Mom insisted on my son coming directly to her house in Orange, meeting me there since I was driving separately in my own car because it had a back seat for Jacob. And so it went; we met at their house in Orange, then drove separately back to Balboa Island. When the visit was over six hours later, we were supposed to deliver Jacob back in separate cars. My son wasn't supposed to go home from my house.

When I arrived and no one answered. I called and begged Jacob's mom to come back explaining that there had been traffic and my son was on his way. Once again I suggested that I drive Jacob to my house. Ah… but that's not what the order said. It seemed rigid, like no coloring over the lines. When my son arrived and I told him what happened, he flipped out, then hung a u-turn and sped away for another two hour drive back to San Diego. I drove home crying.

Another time, my son, had to leave early and went directly home from my house instead of trailing behind my car as I drove Jacob back home. When I dropped Jacob off, his mother was irate about my son not being there. The visits should have been about Jacob, who had always had fun at my house playing on the beach and riding his new two- wheeler with the training wheels around the island. But the unreasonable demands only led to more tension and conflict and the visits were never the same after that. There was always something we did wrong. My son began missing here and there until he eventually gave up. In less than the period of one year everything came apart and by the end of February the court ordered visits stopped. The time, effort and court expense had been futile.

Visiting my grandson on my own was becoming more and more difficult and as I had been reminded by the mom, "I was not a priority."

It had been four months since I had seen Jacob, so when

his third birthday rolled around, I thought surely I would be allowed to see him and deliver his gift. I was wrong. I bought him the nicest toy I could find, a bright yellow plastic car that he could sit in and pedal around.

I was so nervous to visit the apartment that I dragged along my friend, Kathy for moral support. A grandparent herself, Kathy, couldn't understand the cruelty of denying a child a birthday visit from a grandparent.

We walked up to the entrance, stood there for a beat as we listened to party sounds on the other side of the door. Kathy got cold feet and hid behind a wall as I finally mustered up the courage to ring the doorbell. Jacob's mom had just gotten married and when the new husband answered, he had a look of surprise on his face when he saw me standing there with an oversized ride -on yellow car. I asked if I could please give Jacob his gift? He shifted back and forth on his feet, not sure what to do. He glanced over his shoulder as if to defer to Mom. He said he'd ask, as he gently closed the door so that Jacob wouldn't see me.

The door opened a few minutes later when he politely said, "just leave it on the porch," and then closed the door. I reluctantly placed the car with the big red bow on the front step and slowly backed away. I was hoping that I might get a quick glimpse of Jacob but the door never opened. Kathy had no tolerance for such behavior, she fired off profanities about the incident as we walked back to the car. Tears began to roll down my cheeks.

Two days later on Monday morning when I went outside to get the morning newspaper, there sat the yellow car in my front yard. I couldn't believe it.

When I called, Mom's reply was "it's far too extravagant. You should have asked me first."

CHAPTER 5

The Retaliation

THE GIFT REJECTION was the last straw. I decided I better look into grandparent visitation rights as my son's attorney had suggested. After filing the petition, sitting through declarations, and listening to the financial woes of the young couple, I couldn't go through with it. I ended up dropping the case. I simply couldn't put the parents through this. I would have to figure a way to work it out without attorneys.

Even though they were grateful that I stopped the proceedings and ended the lawsuit, the mistrust and hard feelings were still there.

By the time they reluctantly let me start seeing Jacob again, it had been six months, the longest length of time ever that I hadn't seen him. The visiting plan was for me to stop by the apartment and immediately go upstairs to Jacob's room where we played for an hour and then the new husband would give me a holler from downstairs that it was time for me to leave. Mom always made herself scarce, leaving the visit management to the husband. I rarely saw her except when the two of them pressed me to get my son to relinquish his rights so that the new husband would be free to adopt Jacob. That was hard to listen to and I didn't like being put in the position of broker-influencer.

It was getting harder and harder to see my grandson, I felt like I was being squeezed out. First there was the move that took place without a forwarding address or phone number, the Christmas gifts that were eventually delivered in January at the new residence and finally a dinner invite with no dinner and no further hope of communication.

The couple had already eaten when I arrived at the restaurant at the designated time. What was that all about? The meet-up became even more awkward when they announced that they didn't want me seeing Jacob anymore because of the strain on the mom in her condition. She was now pregnant. No amount of reasoning would change their minds. They gave me no assurance that once the baby was born things would go back to the way they were... only a warning that I was not to call them or they would bring a harassment lawsuit against me. Jacob was now three and a half. Time was precious in his young life, which was my biggest concern.

Since I was now clearly banished, I found another attorney who claimed to be an expert in the field of grandparent visitation rights, namedropping previous big cases. I went ahead and filed a petition for visitation, why not, the parents had left me no other choice but to fight for my grandson in order to continue to be a part of his life.

Five months went by without seeing him, and to a child who was used to consistently seeing a loving adult it was too long. For me it was unbearable. The stress was becoming so intense that I sought help from a therapist. His name was Rick Harrison and he was a taskmaster, who both encouraged me to do the work and challenged me when I didn't. He gave me the tools but it was my job to figure out how to use them.

My attorney was eventually able to secure a few visits after the mandatory mediation, which was a wise move on the side of the respondents. The mediation social worker helped the mom and I come to an agreement and the paperwork was forwarded to both attorneys. Twenty- four hours later it came apart when the mom changed her mind. We were now headed for court.

Nothing in the way of a solution came of the hearing, which meant we were headed for trial two weeks later.

Since my attorney had secured temporary visits, the judge hesitated to rule by putting in place a visitation order. She instead, enacted a verbal order requesting that the parents continue to allow me access to my grandchild, otherwise an order would follow. The judge announced, "While I'm not going to rule at this time, I suggest that you work out at least a once per month visitation and if that doesn't happen, then I want to see you back in this courtroom."

As soon as she stated her decision, there was an eruption of cheers from the mom's family. My attorney started to argue, but the judge shut him down along with ordering the family members to knock it off or be in contempt. I was stunned.

After their group left the courtroom, I headed to the elevators along with my attorney. Once we got inside, I let out a wail and threw my head back against the elevator wall and shouted, " How could this happen?" My attorney's response, "This is the first time that I've ever lost a case." All he cared about was his reputation.

I walked around like a zombie for days afterward. Then about two weeks later, I got a call from the new stepdad asking if I'd like to see Jacob? My faith was restored that they were about to comply with the judge's minute order recommendation. I just wanted to see my grandson. It was a Saturday when I arrived only to find that Jacob wasn't there, the parents wanted to have a sit down with me first.

They had some stuff they wanted to get off their chest, which mostly had to do with their financial hardships. An hour later, Jacob was delivered by his maternal grandmother.

The two of us went outside to play street hockey at the end of the cul-de-sac and when it got too hot, we went inside to play board games in his room. We played Hungry Hippo over and over until one of the parents announced that it was time for me to leave. Jacob begged me to stay and didn't understand why I had to go. I hugged him tightly and kissed him goodbye at the front door, not knowing when I would see him again. As I started toward my car, I heard the screen door swing open and as I turned to look over my shoulder, there was Jacob on the porch shouting, "I love you." He was four years old and uttered the words without prompt or as reciprocation. I smiled through happy tears and blew him a kiss before saying, "I love you too." I was on cloud nine all the way home.

I came once a month to play with Jacob enduring the inhospitable environment where his parents kept a close eye on us. At Christmas time I brought a baby gift for the now five month old baby brother. The dad accepted and thanked me and a few minutes later Mom overruled his decision by refusing the gift.

Jacob and I mostly stayed outside and played street hockey, or rather let's see how far Jacob can hit the puck while I chase it.

I always cried all the way home. I was happy to see Jacob but also saddened by the adverse circumstances that felt like a dark cloud hovering overhead. I sometimes felt I was being treated like a pariah with all of the intense scrutiny.

It wasn't long after, that my son signed the papers agreeing to the stepparent adoption. It had been over six months since he had last visited Jacob. His decision was not for me to judge—only he knew what was going on inside himself. My observation was that his life was in a state of chaos and he was struggling. He knew how I felt, but I simply couldn't lobby for continued visits anymore. I could however, continue to be there for Jacob.

I had had a total of nine visits in nine months; seven in person and two by telephone. The last time I saw Jacob was May 5th 2002. My last conversation and the last contact was May 13th by telephone. Period. All remaining scheduled visits were canceled by the parents. An uncle in L.A. was sick. Jacob was sick. They were going out of town. It was always a last- minute excuse.

Three months went by and still no visits. And on August 5th 2002 I received the letter. The parents, stating that they no longer wanted me in Jacob's life, therefore terminating all future visits as a result of a stepparent adoption.

31

They had complied with the visits until the one year waiting period had passed for the adoption. As soon as they had been given the green light following termination of parental rights filing, they filed for stepparent adoption, but since it hadn't been finalized yet they had to comply with the visits under the judge's minute order. They had been married a little over a year and had been on a campaign to get my son, Jacob's biological father to step aside by signing away his rights so that the new dad could adopt Jacob. And now my hands shook as I read the words that I never wanted to see. I fell to my knees and sobbed.

They had been planning this all along was my first thought, even though they promised that I would always be able to see Jacob even after the rights were signed away.

CHAPTER 6

The What Now?

FOLLOWING THE INITIAL shock, I consulted with a new family law attorney who truly did specialize in grandparent rights. She sat across the desk, nose buried in her law book, head bobbing up just long enough to scribble notes on her legal pad. She was seemingly oblivious that there was someone watching her every move. She finally laid the pencil down, closed the book, removed the tortoise readers and gently placed her folded hands on top of her desk. I looked for a sign of optimism. There wasn't one. She explained that according to California law my grandparent visitation rights were terminated along with my son's rights following the stepparent adoption of my grandson. I no longer had standing to petition the court for visitation. It seems once my son gave up his rights, it provided a pathway for the new husband to petition the court to adopt Jacob. Basically, I was no longer recognized in a court of law as Jacob's grandmother.

How could I have gone from Grandma Susan to *persona non grata?* I believed the parents when they said I could continue to see Jacob if I convinced my son to sign the parental termination forms. My son was headed in that direction anyway. He couldn't hack the conflict with Jacob's mother any longer, so it was only a matter of time. I had done my best to prolong the inevitable, but it wasn't my call.

My mistake was getting involved in the first place. Had I not pushed my son to file for visitation, maybe it would have prevented the animosity that going to court produced. It was as if I was seen as a traitor by the mom. Our relationship was never the same after that.

I kept saying to myself that this couldn't be happening, there had to be something I could do. The attorney had a passion for the law and a meaty argument, but compassion for her clients was really what drove her. Which was why it was so hard to tell me that legally she couldn't help me. I shook my head in disbelief, tears flooding my eyes, and through sobs, I said, "No, no, there has to be something you can do, there must be a way?"

The attorney cleared her throat, mischievously raised her eyebrows and said with a smirk, "Actually there are two things you can do: see him on your own in public places and change the law."

I perked up, stifling a sob, "What? What do you mean see him in public places?"

The smirk became a smile, as the attorney explained, "Find out which school he attends, volunteer, go to his soccer games, whatever sports activities he's involved in."

My face brightened as if the "ah ha" moment of discovery had just landed. "So, I need to find a private investigator to find out which school."

"Probably a good idea, just start calling around," said the attorney.

The wheels were turning inside my head. "Just one more thing, what do you mean, change the law?"

"Once your son signed off his rights and the new dad adopted Jacob, your rights went away as well," explained the attorney.

"But that isn't right, how can there be a law that erases a grandparent?"

"I know, but in the eyes of the court you are no longer recognized as his grandparent."

My mouth dropped open in disbelief.

"The idea of grandparent visitation is a fairly new concept and has opposition from parent's rights groups because of a parent's constitutional right to raise their children without interference from government," said the attorney. "It's an uphill battle."

"But, I don't want to interfere with childrearing, I just want to see my grandson and continue the relationship that we have." I interjected. "He won't understand, he'll wonder where I went."

The attorney nodded in agreement, shrugged and said, "And reason for legal reform, unless you want to wait until he's eighteen."

Seeing him on my own covertly was something I could

pursue, changing the law, maybe, but waiting until Jacob is eighteen to see him, was out of the question. Before I followed her suggestions, I asked her about offering the parents money. I would do anything to see him, including pay money to see him. She explained that there were no guarantees, and I could end up throwing the money away. It was a risk I had to take.

A few days later, the attorney made the call to the mother to find out what they wanted. The phone call was long and the attorney's time was costly, but the outcome was hopeful after the attorney listened to the rant about what a despicable person I was and how I had cost her $20,000 in attorney bills... which was how we came up with the amount.

The mom agreed to meet with me. The meeting was arranged to take place on a Sunday morning the following weekend at Alta coffee house in the Cannery Village of Newport Beach.

I was a nervous wreck standing out front waiting. But at 10 a.m., the dad showed up alone. The meeting was friendly, exchanging small talk before moving on to the topic of the payment. At one point I stated, "I want to see Jacob and if paying off your legal fees will help make amends, then I'm willing to do so."

His response was that the decision wasn't his and that he couldn't guarantee that I would get to see Jacob. They needed time to regain trust. It was a risk I would have to take. He showed me a photo of Jacob in a baseball uniform, gave me a hug and said he would be in touch. I had high hopes.

Monday morning I arranged for the funds to be sent. I never heard from either parent again. They cashed the check and that was that. It was a gamble and I knew it.

CHAPTER 7

The Mission

ALL I KNEW was that I wasn't about to wait thirteen years until my grandson turned eighteen to see him. How could I miss watching him growing up? How would I know if he was all right? How would I ever find him after all that time passed if I waited?

During the five years of leaping over hurdles in order to maintain some sort of visit arrangement, the emotional stages of grief had become familiar. I went through the period of gloom and doom, followed by the pleading, the litigation, the bribes, and even pursued legislation. Finally I ventured into uncharted territory.

With option one—waiting until Jacob was eighteen— off the table, two and three—changing the law and seeing him covertly-seemed like logical choices.

My first step was to explore ways to change a law.

Knowing nothing about the California family code, or the legislative system, I had my work cut out for me.

Surely, I could get someone to listen and help me get my grandson back. I looked up the government representatives for my area and then started writing letters and when I didn't get a response, I called. No one would help me, they just kept passing me from one staff member to another and I never got to speak to the real representative. Finally I did manage to get my foot in the door to see my United States Congressman. Name dropping when I called may have helped. His name was Christopher Cox and he listened intently during my fifteen minute appointment as I cried the entire time. His advice: talk to your state assembly or senator because getting a bill about grandparent rights through congress would most likely never happen in this lifetime. The whole thing was confusing, trying to figure out the body of government representatives, who was national and who was local?

Once I figured out who was who, I wrote to them. Then I wrote to some that weren't my representatives, many didn't respond or in some cases I was blocked because I wasn't a constituent. This was time consuming and since I had a full time job I could only work on it during my days off.

Meanwhile I missed Jacob with every fiber inside of me. I felt I needed some professional assistance to figure out a way to see Jacob, maybe at school. I found a private investigator who came highly recommended from a forensic accountant I had once retained. His name was Steve Garrett, just like the Hawaii 5-0 detective. He spent a good amount of time on research and surveillance, and determined that Jacob wasn't attending kindergarten. The best he could figure out was sporadic drop offs at a day care. But with the cul-de-sac obstacle and lack of a set schedule, the investigator suggested we wait until school started. That meant I would have to wait until the fall and try again. A whole year.

One night I couldn't stand it any longer and gave in to the urge to be near him. Doing something is better than doing nothing, I told myself. So I drove to the neighborhood, where I parked on a nearby street and just sat in my car staring out the window at a silver candy wrapper blowing in the breeze. I was frustrated at being so close and coming up empty because there were no viewing spots. I decided to venture out on foot, hiding in the shadows behind Jacob's street. I discovered it led to the 55 freeway just on the other side of the wall at the end of their cul-de-sac. It was a dangerous thing to do, with those cars swooshing past and only some metal fencing between. I took a quick glimpse, saw nothing but a quiet house with no one outside and then ran back down the walkway to the safety of my car.

One Sunday when we were out walking I happened to tell my friend Cherie about my situation and first thing out of her mouth was, "Come on we're going over there, I'll pick you up tonight."

I wanted to do it but I was scared. "How? They'll see us?" I said. "They live on a cul-de-sac and can see every car that drives down the street."

"Just leave it to me, trust me, OK?"

I was so desperate I agreed. I would do anything to see him.

That night Cherie picked me up in her silver Chevy Suburban and we headed up to Orange. First we did a drive-by via the cross street that bordered the end of the cul-de-sac and that's when we noticed an early model white Ford Explorer with a "For Sale" sign in the window. It was parked in the curve of the dead end street that was in front of the house where Jacob lived. Cherie, who had no fear of anything and was the gutsiest person I knew, said, "Climb in the very back and lay down."

"Ok but what if they see me?"

"Just do it, the interior is dark and windows are tinted, so don't worry about it."

I squeezed between the driver and passenger front seat opening into the back seat and then heaved myself over the back into the cargo area where I pressed myself flat on the floor.

Cherie turned onto the street and cruised slowly toward the end where the white SUV was parked. Looking straight ahead, she said, "If someone comes over, I'll tell them I'm looking at the "For Sale" information, now stay down."

She stopped in front of the SUV and I risked a quick peek, and there was the dad and another man sitting in lawn chairs talking and drinking beer. I saw Cherie give her long black hair a flick over her shoulder before she checked herself in the rearview mirror. Then she said, "Here he comes." Now I was really terrified as I tried to make myself invisible.

She rolled down the window and no doubt gave the dad one of her 100 watt smiles accentuating her deep dimples, "Hi, is that your car?"

It was but he was curious about how she had known about the car being for sale. Quick on her feet, she invented a falsehood about taking a wrong turn, getting lost in the neighborhood. Satisfied, he then started explaining about the car and why he was selling it.

She embellished her story a little more, saying, "Oh, it's not for me, it's for my brother, who lives in San Diego. I'm helping him look for a car…blah, blah, blah." She retrieved a paper and pen from her purse and wrote down the dad's number along with the pertinent technical details about the vehicle.

I thought the conversation would never end. I was still worried he was going to bust us, even though Cherie was so convincing that I almost believed her myself. As soon as he turned to walk back to join his friend, Cherie said, "Sit up, there's a little boy at the screen door, is that Jacob?"

Sure enough, there he was, standing there in his P.J.'s, peering out the front door. The Suburban made a slow a U-turn so I could take another quick peek before I had to duck as we passed by the two men, but my 30 second glimpse was better than what I'd had, which had been nothing.

Once we cleared the street and I climbed back into the front seat I started breathing again. It was a risky encounter. I said to Cherie, who was cool as a cucumber, "I can't believe you just did that, weren't you even a little nervous?" She just laughed.

Although this was emotionally draining and the scariest thing I've ever done, I knew I had to somehow do it again. Maybe after the investigator figured out Jacob's school situation, there would be a way to see him without being visible? That house location was definitely not user friendly for spying.

Cherie, always thinking outside the box, came up with a wild idea that maybe I should try to buy the house behind them, that way I could see him as often as I wanted. I wouldn't have discounted anything at that point.

The covert option given me by the attorney as a way to see Jacob was going to be my course of operation. All I knew was that I had to see him, even if I couldn't touch him or let him know that I was there and hadn't abandoned him.

I reasoned, if I couldn't have an interdependent relationship, then at least I could keep track of him, his growth and watch over him from afar. But first I had to figure out how? As long as my surveillance was in a public place, and discreet, I wouldn't be breaking any laws. If I got sloppy and was caught a restraining order would surely be a consequence.

Just after Labor Day, I contacted Steve the investigator and asked if he could try to find which school Jacob was enrolled in. This time he had success when he learned that Jacob was, indeed, enrolled in school. After I received all of the detailed information, I made an unusual request, which was to tag along on the stakeout. He said that wasn't usually done, and that he had never taken a client along. Not being deterred, I persisted and Steve finally agreed to meet me at the last exit on the 55 freeway just before the 91 freeway where there was a strip mall.

There was one detail I had to take care of before I met up with the investigator. I'd passed by the tiny store called "Wigs" on Pacific Coast Highway a million times, but this was the first time I had set foot inside. I took a deep breath as I stepped through the front door of the tiny store. I began to feel overwhelmed with all of the faceless styrofoam heads displaying every hair color and style imaginable. I became even more self-conscious when the owner approached to ask what I wanted a wig for. The first words that tumbled out of my mouth were, "Uh, um I'm thinking of changing my hair color and I thought I would try a wig first." Some might view going to such lengths as crazy, but I didn't care, I had to cover all the bases.

After trying on a collection of styles, I settled on a dark blond highlighted shaggy style that wouldn't draw too much attention.

Tuesday afternoon, with my new wig covering my familiar dark brown hair, I cautiously pulled into the strip mall feeling paranoid. My eyes scanned the parking lot to make sure no one was around that I knew, mainly the parents. Somewhat satisfied that I wouldn't run into them, I made my way over to the tan truck that the investigator had described. Steve hopped out and we introduced ourselves and then I climbed into the passenger side of his truck and off we went to the private Christian school just a few miles away.

We pulled into the parking lot before school let out and instead of getting in the pick- up line, we eased into a parking space and then sat in the truck to watch and wait. After a few minutes, I had a thought and slid out of the car and decided to go onto school property so I could get a better view of Jacob on my own. It was still early, before parents had begun to arrive, and I felt somewhat certain that I could blend in. The detective waited in the car while I threw my purse over my shoulder and boldly walked onto the campus, praying that I wouldn't run into Mom or Dad.

With the wig of a different color and style than my own hair, the big sunglasses, baggy clothes and an air of confidence that I truly didn't have but was part of my act, I behaved like

I belonged there. I eased myself onto a bench at the outdoor picnic table area where some parents had gathered waiting for their kids to be released from class.

A few minutes later, multiple doors began to open and kids emerged from classrooms all at once following teachers in a straight line. Uh oh, this was not good; they all looked alike, same height, same uniforms, and lots of dark haired boys. Not knowing which room he was coming from how was I going to pick him out from the crowd? Then I thought of something that would help me spot him quickly, his foot. There were so many kids but that foot would distinguish him from the others. He was pigeon toed, with his right foot turning in more than his left, so I focused on each of the kids' legs as they walked from their classrooms to the front of the school where the cars were beginning to line up.

First I saw the foot, then I raised my eyes upward and sure enough, that was Jacob. I exhaled and smiled to myself as I watched him make his way to the pick up location in front of the school. I was stuck now until he was picked up because I couldn't risk being seen when I walked back across the parking lot. I stayed put, grateful for the few minutes I had to be close to Jacob as he stood directly in front of me on the other side of the blue slatted metal fence, not three feet from where I sat. He was wearing khaki shorts and a green polo shirt like everyone else and I couldn't help notice the dark hair on the back of his little legs. A few minutes later, the carpool teacher on duty approached a big silver truck, opened the door and signaled for Jacob placing him in the back seat. Off he went.

As soon as it pulled away, I safely made my exit and once

I was back in the car, I made another request to the detective, "can we follow that car, please, and see where they go?" With a nod, Steve quickly maneuvered his way out of the lot amongst all of the chaos and began tailing the truck a few blocks until they pulled into a Trader Joe's. I wanted a photo but I wasn't about to go inside and have them see me, so this time I stayed in the car. Steve had an idea, which was to pretend he was a photographer shooting photos of the store sign in front. I watched with fascination as he put on a show with his camera and pen and pad, like he was surveying something. Sure enough about ten minutes later, Mom, Dad, Jacob, and little brother sitting in the child seat of the shopping cart, headed right to where Steve was standing.

After fourteen months, a sense of relief came over me now that I finally got to see him and felt satisfied that he was fine. Steve promised to send the photo as soon as he had it developed.

CHAPTER 8

The Activist

THE JACOB SIGHTING kept me going for a while but everyday was still a struggle to adapt to a life without him. While I did my best to focus on other things in my life, like my job, the hole in my heart grew deeper.

My obsession with his school website was just another way to bring me closer to him. Just about everyday I checked for photos. In October, there was a school photo commemorating September 11th where the entire school posed for a photo in the shape of a flag. I spent hours zooming in and then using a magnifier so I could pick Jacob out from a few hundred kids all dressed alike. I was pretty sure that I located him in the second row, at least I convinced myself it was him.

In the mean time, I continued my research on grandparent visitation issues. That's how I came up with an idea to circulate a petition in favor of grandparent rights to Orange County residents. My thinking was that this would get the legislators' attention once I delivered a stack of signed petitions from concerned citizens to them.

I found a petition template online, printed off about 100 pages, attached them to a clipboard and then solicited a friend to help me walk the neighborhood. Jill, who was an apparel model mostly working in boutiques and restaurants, was used to talking to strangers. She was outgoing and friendly which is exactly what I needed to give me the courage to approach people I didn't know.

We set off together on a Saturday, walking along the boardwalk near the Newport Beach pier. I followed her lead as she confidently approached strangers in the beach parking lot and sidewalk, even speaking Spanish to some. At one point she brazenly walked into one of the dive bars, Blackies, that lined the parking lot and grabbed a few signatures.

The next day was Sunday and she had to work in one of the boutiques in Lido Village but not until she escorted me into the Elks Club where they were serving Sunday brunch to about 50 members. She introduced me to the piano playing entertainer and asked if he would let me say a few words to the crowd before asking them for signatures.

I grabbed her arm and protested, saying, "Jill no, I can't do that. Why can't you ask them?"

She smiled, saying, "I have to be at work in five minutes, c'mon don't worry, you'll be fine, everyone here is super nice and Benny will help you as soon as as he finishes his song."

I stood against a wall a few feet from the piano holding my clipboard against my chest like a protective shield, not quite knowing what to do with myself as everyone was filling their plates from the buffet and socializing at tables in the waterfront facility.

Benny ended his song and motioned me over with his hand so he could get some details about what I was all about. I gave him the edited version of the issue and he told me to sit tight and as soon as the members were all seated he would make the announcement. He sang a few more songs and as his set was ending, he told the attendees, who all looked like grandparents, that he wanted them to meet a young lady who had a message and a request for support in the way of signing a petition.

He handed me the mic and I began to tell my story. After the first few words, with the emotions still raw, I started crying. Somehow I stumbled through it finally asking the audience if they would lend their support by signing my petition. They actually clapped as I handed Benny the mic and made my way over to the tables where I circulated my petition. As I passed around the clipboard, some of the people began asking me specific questions, some shared, some said nothing but everyone signed.

The following Saturday Jill canceled on me. It was my day off and I wanted to make good use of my time getting signatures but I didn't want to go alone. I called my dad. He suggested Mile Square Park in Fountain Valley, which was near his house, and so we met there.

It was around lunchtime and a good time to find families gathering for picnics. We wandered around for a while looking for approachable people. I was even more reluctant to walk up to strangers than before because my dad wasn't as outgoing as Jill and I had to be the leader this time.

It was hard, randomly walking up to strangers, but every time we received positive feedback, it became a little easier. We approached a large Hispanic family having a picnic and who barely spoke English. They offered us food and then money, which I couldn't accept although it touched my heart. Their kindness gave me the confidence to keep going.

An experience I will never forget was the Vietnamese gathering. There must have been close to a hundred people celebrating an annual reunion because they were originally from the same village in Vietnam. Most of them were sitting on a small hill in the shade eating the ethnic food that they had just prepared, and when we approached they invited us to sit down and eat with them as they passed around the clipboard. I sat with them as my dad stood close-by watching the interaction unfold.

We had been out there all afternoon, navigating the huge park and by four o'clock we were hot, tired and hungry. I was grateful that I had made some progress and also for the time with my father even though it was an unusual outing.

The next day I roped my 21 year old daughter into coming with me to Main Beach in Laguna Beach. There are always lots of people milling around the compact beach that sits on Pacific Coast Highway across from the downtown village, making it easier to cover more territory in a shorter period of time.

My daughter opted for the bench instead of walking with me as I talked to strangers. She was clearly embarrassed.

This made me feel anxious at first but after I started getting signatures, it got a little less stressful.

After two weekends of gathering signatures from strangers combined with the stack I had gotten from friends and family, I ended up with a few hundred. My plan was to take them to a legislator as documentation that I had support.

I contacted my local assemblyman and he agreed to see me, the only problem was I had to go to Sacramento if I wanted a meeting during the current term before the deadline for bill introduction. I was scheduled to meet with Ken Maddox of Costa Mesa, then a friend recommended that as long as I was up there I should meet with a Santa Barbara legislator with whom she was a constituent and felt that she would be sympathetic to grandparents since she was one.

I flew to Sacramento and back in the same day. I had never been to the state capitol before, let alone met with a state legislator. Armed with a briefcase full of petitions, I met with Assemblyman Maddox shortly after the cab dropped me off in the morning. He was nice enough, but after fifteen minutes he explained that his bill package was nearly full and if not this year then we should revisit the issue the following year. He said he would give it some thought and would get back to me.

I got directions to the cafeteria and ate lunch while I waited for the two o'clock appointment. Hannabeth Jackson was unavailable to meet with me in-person, so I met with her assistant, a lankly young man who couldn't have been more aloof. I took him a gift of gourmet nuts. He said they weren't supposed to accept gifts, but he took them anyway.

I pitched my message, showed him all of my petitions of support, answered all of his questions and after 30 minutes, he said, sorry it's not something we'd be interested in carrying. Boom, just like that no discussion.

When I got up to leave, he said, with a smirk on his face, " Do you want to take your gift back now?"

Holding back tears, I responded, "Of course not."

I made a beeline to the first restroom I found and broke down and called my friend Dr. Lillian Carson, a grandparent advocate, and author on the subject. She had referred me to Assembly woman Jackson. Sobbing, I said, "That guy was so cocky and arrogant he couldn't care less about grandparents."

Lillian seemed taken aback, asking, "I don't understand, didn't you get to see Hannabeth?"

"No, just her assistant," I said through choking sobs.

I repeated what he said about not wanting to pursue legislation on behalf of grandparent right's laws.

"He let me sit there and carry on all that time for nothing, he knew all along they weren't going to get involved."

Lillian did her best to console me and then I left the capitol building and looked for something to do for three hours before my flight at 6 o'clock. I found a shopping mall nearby where I wandered around for awhile until I got hungry and set out to find a restaurant. It had started raining so I ducked into a small bistro where I sat alone at a tall table near the window in the bar area and ate my dinner. I gazed out the window at the deserted dark street pummeled by the steady sheets of rain, poking at my food and trying to blink away tears.

CHAPTER 9

The Support

FEELING DEJECTED AND like a complete failure I began searching the internet for grandparent organizations that may be able to provide support and information. I found Grandparents R Us, which was more of a support network than a traditional organization. The woman who ran it was religious and communicated that theme into her practice. She became someone I could count on for support as well as insight whenever we spoke on the phone. She gave me ideas about how to establish my own group and organization whenever I was ready. In the mean time, she even offered to give me a page on her website until I could create one of my own.

The other grandparent group was actually a non-profit organization called GRACE (Grandparents and Children Embrace) and was run by Jean Castagno of Connecticut. She had been active in the grandparent movement for several years and became an invaluable source of information and support for me. She had a good understanding of the laws and the workings of legislation and experience with grandparent problems. And yes, she was also a disenfranchised grandparent.

I was able to meet Jean in person when she invited me to be a participant in a shared panel discussion at a CRC (Children's Rights Council) conference in Washington DC in November of 2003. I agreed, with reluctance, not quite understanding what it was all about. Once I arrived, though, Jean took me under her wing. The first day of the three-day conference we took the train into the DC metro area and she showed me around inside the Capitol where we sat in on a member of congress in the midst of a filibuster. We walked around the city where she pointed out the landmarks and some senate offices before we stopped off at the AARP office. We didn't have an appointment but left a message with the staff requesting a call.

The next day we attended the keynote speaker seminar in the morning, followed by our panel at one o'clock that afternoon.

It was in a smaller meeting room that held around 25 people. There was three of us at the speaker table, and Jean went first, followed by a woman named Lola Bailey and then me.

When it was my turn, as I began to read my written speech about my situation of losing access to my grandson, my struggle to get through it was clearly evident. I choked on my sobs and my eyes were so clouded with tears that I could barely see the words on the paper. Of course I knew my own story, but public speaking was not something I was used to and not only did I have a bad case of stage fright, the grief and emotions were still raw whenever I spoke about it.

The audience politely clapped when I was finished, and then they started asking questions to each of us. As I stood to leave, a handful of attendees approached me with more questions specific to my situation.

That night I joined Jean and her husband for dinner where we said our good byes. I loved meeting and spending time with Jean, but left feeling no closer to finding a way to cope, let alone helping others.

CHAPTER 10

The New Way Of Life

THE HOLIDAYS WERE especially hard because I wasn't allowed to send Christmas gifts to Jacob. Instead, I bought gifts for kids in foster care and delivered them to Orangewood Children's Center on Christmas Eve. It gave me comfort knowing a child in need would have a gift for Christmas.

Jacob was always on my mind. I continued to work out different ways to see him without anyone knowing—including him. During one of my school website searches looking for photos, I discovered that there were some field trips coming up in February 2004. That's when a light bulb went on in my head. After further digging, I came upon a posted schedule of upcoming trips for his grade. It looked like the two first grade classrooms were planning a group whale-watching excursion from Davey's Locker in a few days. Too good to be true, since the Newport Harbor was practically in my back yard.

I contacted the excursion boating office to confirm the times after I saw the posted itinerary on the school site. The next thing I did was solicit one of my work friends to come with me. After I sold the store I'd run for thirteen years I went to work as a pro-shop buyer at a golf country club, which is where I became friends with Richard. I had cried on his shoulder many times, and although he wasn't a grandparent, he had compassion for my situation. He was from a large close knit family where everyone respected one another, especially the grandparents.

It was my day off so I picked up Richard in the parking lot of the country club around lunchtime after he finished his shift. I waited in my car since I was wearing my wig and didn't want to face my work pals and their questions.

Richard and I arrived just as the tour boat was docking and watched from the boardwalk as the kids began to exit down the ramp toward the fun zone area. There were a ton of kids from several different schools. I finally spotted Jacob's group, who were all dressed in khaki pants and navy or green polo shirts bearing the school logo.

The teachers corralled the kids and led them toward the beach and the Balboa Pier. Richard and I followed not far behind so I could get a better view of Jacob. The kids were paired up and holding hands with each other as they walked to the end of the Balboa pier and back. It was when we were following within two feet of Jacob and his walking buddy, that I managed to snap a quick photo of the two little six-year-old boys holding hands and laughing.

From there the group of children headed to the grassy area

near the parking lot where they ran and played. I sat on the grass and watched as Richard shot a few photos of me with my little sure-shot 35 mm camera as I watched Jacob play.

I could have sat there all day and watched him play. It was a bittersweet afternoon; I was happy to see Jacob, but sad that it had come to this and he would never know that I was there.

The field trip episode most likely wasn't going to be an isolated incident. It only provided positive reinforcement for me to do it again. If I could pull it off once, why not again? And again? That's when I decided that I needed a camera with a long lens so that I could not only document my trips but do so at a safe distance.

CHAPTER 11

The Field Trips

IT ALL STARTED to come together when I stepped up to the display counter at the camera store and said to the salesmen, "Give me a camera with the biggest lens you have." He gave me a quizzical look before he began peppering me with technical questions, which of course I couldn't answer. But when he asked what I was planning to use it for? I stammered something about getting close-ups at my kids' sporting events. It didn't take a genius to figure out that my camera knowledge didn't go any further than a point and shoot device. Finally I settled on a professional type digital camera with a 200 millimeter zoom lens that was an intimidating piece of equipment. It didn't matter how much it cost or that I didn't understand the first thing about operating a real camera, I was on a mission and I needed tools. I'd figure it out along the way.

Now armed with a decent camera, and a pretty good disguise, I planned my next venture. It had been two months since the fun zone and once again I called upon Richard. This time he had his seven month old baby with him, so we drove to a park in Irvine that I had seen on the field trip schedule. We walked around, like a normal family, him pushing the stroller with the baby and me walking beside. This time it was a dead end. Either the trip was somewhere else or it had been canceled, because there wasn't a group of kids anywhere. We drove around Mason Park, which was huge, and never did see any groups of kids. Richard was a good sport and it was fun having his baby daughter along for the ride, but still I was disappointed.

Sure there would be other field trip opportunities, but in the mean time I had to pacify myself. The next day, I decided to take a trip to the school just to be closer to Jacob and if I got lucky maybe see him playing on the playground.

I got the bright idea to borrow a car from a car dealer friend under the pretense of a test drive. The only problem with the car was the color, it was a cobalt blue and didn't exactly blend in. Served me right, I suppose, for trying to pull a stunt like that. I may or may not have seen Jacob among the kids on the playground that day. It didn't matter, making the trip made me feel like I was at least doing something. The next time I decided to do a school drive-by, I rented a car, and that time it produced a sighting of an after school pick up.

In the meantime, I continued to visit the school website looking for upcoming classroom outings.

Sure enough the next one was in May at the Oak Canyon Nature Center in Anaheim. I didn't know what that was, but didn't let that stop me. This time I was on my own.

After making a few laps around the facility, I parked on the street in a residential neighborhood where I kept looking in the rearview mirror to make sure no one saw me as I pulled the hairnet over my long hair and pinned it tightly to my scalp before placing the wig over it. I took some deep breaths to calm my nerves, then exited my car and walked a few blocks to the center.

It was filled with kids running around, and it would take me a while to locate Jacob's school group by their uniforms.

I was traipsing around the hills when I caught a glimpse of a group of kids in a grassy area below. It looked like they were part of a guided tour out exploring the ecology and plant community that was in the natural 58 acre park in the Anaheim Hills. Even though they were pretty far away, I clicked off a few photos anyway —just in case.

It was hard to blend in—a woman alone with a camera. When I noticed the kids heading toward the buildings I kept a wide berth and followed from a safe distance. It turned out to be an interpretive center with exhibits of reptiles, insects and birds. How was I going to take photographs singling out one child without it being weird? My solution: pretend like I'm taking pictures of the critters in the glass aquariums. I waited until I saw Jacob viewing something inside a display and that's when I shot the photos through the glass.

The pictures turned out blurry or contained obstacles, like twigs and rocks that blocked a clear view of Jacob, but it was the only way and better than nothing.

I hit the jackpot with the next field trip opportunity.

Summertime was all about day camp that included weekly field trips to the beach, baseball games, theme parks and just about any activity to entertain kids. My interest was the beach since the majority of the trips were to Corona del Mar State Beach, which was close by my house.

The school provided a summer camp schedule. Every time they went to Big Corona, I went as well. I didn't know if he would be there, but I went anyway and once I spotted the yellow school buses in the parking lot, I trekked down to the sand hoping I would see him. Sometimes I did and sometimes I didn't. And whenever I did, I set up my beach chair and settled in like any other beach goer. Once settled, I pulled my camera from my tote bag and viewed him through the lens. I was perfectly content just to be close by and watch him dig holes in the sand and play with the other kids in the water.

When December of the same year rolled around, the class was scheduled to attend the live performance of Joseph And The Amazing Dreamcoat at the Huntington Beach High School Historic Auditorium. I couldn't believe it, that was my high school. I checked and double checked the High School website to get more information before making the trip. I even called to confirm seating, saying something like, "hi, I just wanted to ask about seating for the grandparents."

My greatest fear was that I would run into the mom, as a helper on one of these field trips, which made me even more of a nervous wreck. But, once I entered the auditorium, I had to act as though I belonged there. In reality it was de-ja- vu, since I hadn't set foot on the campus since I graduated. Of all the places in Orange County, my high school was the venue.

There was a sea of big yellow school buses from many different schools jockeying for a curbside slot. This was going to be a challenge.

Once I made it inside without incident, I noticed a few rows of kids already seated. That's when I began strolling up and down the aisles looking for the right uniform for Jacob's school. Then I noticed the balcony, so I ran up the stairs and checked out the group up there. I thought to myself, how am I going to monitor the balcony and main level? It was when three quarters of the auditorium quickly filled up with one school after another that I panicked and figured I had either somehow missed seeing him, or he wasn't coming. With the play set to begin in just under ten minutes, I grabbed a seat in one of the two remaining empty rows toward the back and fixated on the open door where stragglers were still entering.

Then I saw the line of kids dressed in khaki and green uniforms quickly advancing toward the empty row in front of where I sat. One by one I looked over at each dark haired boy until I saw Jacob. There he was, I held my breath as I watched each child making their way down the long center row before they sat, closer, closer. When Jacob found his seat it was directly in front of me. Whew. Thank you lord.

He briefly glanced over his shoulder before he settled into his seat and then paid more attention to the little boy next to him. As the lights dimmed, I saw him turn around again to see who was behind him just before the play began. It was a quick glance without any indication of recognition.

I was happy just to be able to sit inches away from him and if it meant staring at the back of his head that was fine with me. I caught a glimpse of his profile a few times whenever he whispered to his buddy, but mostly it was the back of his head. I was so close it was all I could do to keep from touching him. Just one little pat on his head, wouldn't hurt, would it?

An hour later the lights came on once the show ended, which by the way was wasted on me since my entertainment had consisted of concentrating on Jacob and not what was on stage.

Everyone stood by their seat as they waited for the theater to empty row by row, front to back before filing out. That gave me more time to enjoy my close proximity and watch Jacob interact with his classmates. As his row exited with mine closely behind, it was easy to find him outside playing with other kids under the teacher's supervision. I used the opportunity to whip out my camera now that I had lots of light and start snapping some quick photos. I kept my eye peeled on the teacher to make sure she wasn't watching this woman taking photos of the kids in her classroom.

I checked her out to see where she was looking each time before I clicked the shutter, and if she glanced in my direction, I either pretended to be taking photos of the building or I would place the camera by my side. She was so focused on managing the children I don't think she noticed me. I probably could have aimed the lens right at her and she wouldn't have seen it. But I wasn't taking any chances. Happily, I did get some cute shots of Jacob interacting with his schoolmates outside the school before they boarded the bus. Once I completed my mission, I nonchalantly made my way to the parking lot with a smile on my face. I felt so fortunate to have been able to sit so close to him. Sure as crazy as it was, I wanted to reach over and touch him, but this was a satisfying compromise. And when I think of all of the seats in that theater, it truly was miraculous that he ended up right in front of me.

CHAPTER 12

Taking It Up A Notch

CHRISTMAS WAS ALWAYS a difficult reminder that I no longer had my grandson to buy for. The toys that would have been for Jacob and now went to foster children at Orangewood did help ease the pain of not being able to celebrate the holiday in some way with him.

As soon as the holidays were out of the way, it was time to get back into the business of daily field trip schedule checking for the spring semester. The next one that popped up was a trip to the Los Angeles Zoo, which was not only over an hour away but was scheduled two weeks after my foot surgery. I was going no matter what.

I started thinking that preserving Jacob's voice would be nice. I was missing so much and to able to hear his voice as he grew older was important to me. This time I went to a different store and bought a compact Canon video camera, which was actually a lot simpler to operate than my still camera.

I hadn't been to the zoo in decades and once I passed through the gates of the massive property — 133 acres — I became concerned that I would never find him. I roamed around, keeping my eyes peeled for a group of kids wearing uniforms. Sure enough, in front of one of the mammal exhibit areas, was Jacob and another boy accompanied by a parent. I pulled my wide brimmed straw hat lower on my forehead, took a deep breath, and stepped up to the fence. Trying not to be conspicuous, I removed my video camera from the case with an air of confidence I didn't have and applying a firm grip, aimed it at the animals.

With the camera pressed up against my face, I eased closer to where Jacob and his group were standing so I could eavesdrop. The parent belonged to the other boy and he was explaining the facts listed on the descriptive sign about the different Duiker species. The boys were jumping around and didn't seem that interested. Even though I was wearing sunglasses, a big sunhat with my wig underneath, I always kept the camera close to my face as if I was about to record another shot. After a few minutes passed, it just seemed natural for me to join in the conversation, so I did. I mean I was there all by myself and had no one to talk to, so I chimed in whenever appropriate. Saying stuff like, " I didn't know that there were so many varieties from the antelope family." That would then get the dad responding. "Oh yeah there's… according to the description."

"They sure seem oblivious to us watching them."

"Yeah, the boys tried to get them to come to the fence but they pretty much ignored them."

They eventually wandered off toward the next display and I casually followed, now feeling the foot pain and doing my best not to limp. Following my foot surgery I was supposed to be wearing a boot on my sore foot, but I thought it would call too much attention, so I crammed my foot into a sneaker, which was killing me because the foot was still swollen. I didn't want to find a place to sit and take the chance that I would lose sight of them so I clenched my teeth trying to keep a close distance behind them.

After about thirty minutes of following, they hopped on a tram and—grateful to finally sit down—so did I. After the short ride they headed for the gift shop as did I. Zoo themed souvenirs were abundant, so I bought myself a tee shirt with the zoo logo and a lion stenciled on the front, not because it was that great, but because it would be a reminder of this day every time I wore it. After two hours, I hobbled to the parking lot, this time not caring who saw me limp, and made the long drive home.

I couldn't wait to plug my camera into my computer so I could watch my recording. This was my first experience shooting video and I had no idea what I was doing. All I knew was to aim the lens directly at Jacob and hold it still while he did the moving around. The movie footage was rough but I didn't care, now I could hear his voice and play it back anytime I wanted to hear him.

Three months later in May, the class listed the Fullerton Arboretum for their next trip.

The Fullerton Arboretum is a 26 acre botanical garden

located on the northeast corner of the Cal. State Fullerton University campus.

This time I had to park on the premises in order to access the facility. It was a public venue and seemed to be bustling with activity from students, individual visitors and tours, always a good thing to help me blend in. Once I got the lay of the land, I spotted Jacob and classmates sitting on the oversized porch of an 1894 Eastlake-style house from the Victorian era that was painted in a dark yellow with scrolls, lattice, and carvings. It was called Heritage House and apparently docents dressed in Victorian dress led historic tours of the restored house, and gardens. The house and other historic structures served as a museum of family life and medical practice in the 1890's that included an outhouse and windmill in the yard. The vintage backdrop made a perfect setting for a photo. There were no teachers around so I freely clicked off a series of shots of the four little boys messing around on the front steps of the ornate house.

Since there were no more trips listed on the website for the rest of the year, it was back to summer camp. Camp had proven to be the easiest access in the past, but the downside was that I had no way of knowing if Jacob would be going. During the school year it was a given, but summertime activities were optional at the camp.

Whenever I visited the beach the previous summer, Jacob was usually there so I felt confident that would be the case when I decided one day to bring my dad along so that he could see Jacob. He had only seen him twice, once as a newborn and again as a toddler. We parked on Ocean Avenue in Corona del

Mar and walked down the steep hill to the beach. We then headed toward the sand looking for large groups of elementary school age kids. I spotted the royal blue tee shirts that some of the boys were wearing and there he was amongst them, digging a hole. The previous half dozen times I had seen him, he had always been digging in the sand, something he clearly loved to do when he was at the beach.

Once I pointed him out to my dad, he lowered his voice and asked if he could go talk to him? I'm not sure if he was kidding, but I adamantly shook my head and said, "absolutely not."

He nonchalantly drifted over and stood about two feet from where Jacob was busily digging and observed the activity. He looked harmless to anyone passing by, just a nice grandpa casually strolling the beach and stopping briefly to watch the kids play. I snapped a couple of photos and then signaled for him to come back so it wouldn't arouse suspicion.

As we climbed back up the hill shortly after our quick peek, we chatted about how much he had grown and how cute he was. My dad had driven over with the sole purpose of meeting up so he could see his great-grandson. Mission accomplished.

CHAPTER 13

The Call

IT WAS AUGUST of 2005 when I got the call from Jacob's adoptive dad. I had been reading in bed when the phone rang around nine o'clock.

His first words, "she's doing to me what she did to you." I was stunned to hear his voice at the other end of the phone. He sounded distraught and after a few minutes into the conversation, he began to weep.

He explained that Jacob's mom had thrown him out and wanted a divorce. I listened as he proceeded to tell me the details of their marriage woes. He said several times, "I'm sorry for keeping Jacob away from you, and I'm going to make sure that you see him right away."

I said, "as much as I want to see him after three years, maybe we should wait until you go to court."

He wouldn't hear of it and repeatedly said that he wanted me to see Jacob.

I had a bad feeling that if he flaunted the idea to the mom that it would open a great big can of worms.

The conversation was hard, here was one of the parents who had prevented me from seeing my grandson and who was now crying and pouring his heart out about his wife.

He said he wanted to meet with me the next day, but I never heard from him. About a week later I called him to find out what was going on, and he said that he did in fact tell the mom that he was going to let me see Jacob and that she went ballistic. I couldn't help but wonder about that.

The thought crossed my mind about the dad's motivation? If the mom believed that by leaving her husband, I would then be back in Jacob's life, maybe she would reconsider and not divorce after all. I didn't want to think about it, I knew he was desperate. I pushed those thoughts from my mind. I just wanted to see Jacob and believed that his dad would keep his promise.

A couple of weeks later, I met the dad for iced tea at the Orange circle, where he had just met with a family law attorney. The attorney agreed that we should wait until the dust settles before arranging a visit. In other words a legal separation had to be filed first before the dad could start making plans that were unilateral.

My concession was that I had waited three years, so another month or so wouldn't make much difference. That and the fact that I had been seeing him secretly on my own anyway eased my anxiety.

The timing was ironic as I had just arranged my first grandparent support group in Laguna Beach, where I had been living for the past year. It didn't matter that I could very well be seeing Jacob in the near future, the grandparent alienation issue was still important and I would never forget the grief and suffering and the unbearable pain. I decided no matter the outcome for me personally, I wanted to help others. No one understands what it feels like to lose access to a grandchild unless they have experienced it.

I didn't know how many other grandparents were experiencing similar alienation, but I had a feeling that it could become a growing social problem and if so, grandparents needed all the help they could get.

The notice that I'd placed in the local newspaper soliciting interest for a support group drew three callers. The Laguna Beach American Legion generously donated a room and we had our first meeting about a week after the ad ran. In attendance were a local couple and two other men.

This was my first experience as a facilitator for a support group and I decided to just be myself and talk to the other grandparents like I would to a friend. After introducing ourselves, I suggested that each one of us share why we were there. The couple, Earl and Linda, also had a grandson named Jacob, which instantly connected us. Their son and daughter-in-law abruptly moved to another state cutting off all communication. What was perplexing was that there had been no argument or disagreement to trigger the situation. They simply dropped out of site and cut off all family ties without explanation.

One of the men shared that he wasn't getting along with his daughter because of her new boyfriend, but he was still able to visit his granddaughter. The other man was thinking about retaining legal counsel and wanted to discuss the laws.

Toward the end of the meeting, Earl excused himself and walked outside where he began pacing, never returning. He had been closer than anyone to his firstborn grandson and was taking the separation hard. Linda and I easily communicated and developed a camaraderie. She welcomed the supportive connection and was enthusiastic about continuing the group meetings every month.

About six months after the Laguna Beach meetings began I moved to Corona del Mar and transferred the location to OASIS Senior Center in Corona del Mar. The city of Newport Beach sponsored us by giving us usage of one of the classrooms at no charge. They also listed us on the resource page of the newsletter that included us in the City Of Newport Beach quarterly class offerings, under support services.

The new location drew more attendees, averaging ten or so each month from as far as San Diego; we were off to a good start providing a service to the community.

As for seeing Jacob, I waited until all of the legal requirements were satisfied and the dad's attorney gave the ok. During the two months that I was waiting I became better acquainted with Jacob's dad and his family. It was on a Saturday when I was invited to the new house that he had rented in Orange for himself and the boys, whenever they visited. When I arrived, he was busy doing repairs and didn't want me to wait around for him to finish, so he suggested that I go visit his mom who lived a few blocks away. He had mentioned that she had found the house for him after a neighbor had told her about it. I felt a little weird barging in on her, but he insisted and said she was expecting me. I had only seen her one time when she and her husband and another grandchild dropped by while I was playing with Jacob in his front yard. That day, I had just brought a robot toy for the then three- year-old Jacob and we were trying to put it together when the dad's family drove up. His stepdad made a point of coming over to introduce himself. At the time, I was already an outcast and was restricted to outside playtime and only at his house. The other child they had brought with them came over to see what we were doing and Jacob showed no interest in playing with her. He was focused on the new toy and on only one person, me.

This time would be different, since we were all on the same side now. I arrived ten minutes later to a tree-lined street filled with large traditional homes with big front yards. His mom welcomed me into her home with a warm and friendly greeting. She had the same grandchild there who was now swimming in the pool with a friend. The girl had to be at least ten by now. She ushered me to the kitchen so that she could keep an eye on the girls. The first thing she said, when I sat across from her at the kitchen table was, "Jacob looks exactly like you."

She then said, "You're part of the family." She proceeded to invite me to celebrate Halloween, which was just around the corner and something they made a big deal out of. Thanksgiving and Christmas were also included in the invite.

The warm welcome into their family was a pleasant surprise and brought me that much closer to Jacob.

The next time I visited the dad, he and his mom were getting the house ready for the kids to come for their first court ordered visit. It seems I wasn't the only one denied visitation. Apparently Jacob's mom had kept the boys from seeing the dad with a temporary restraining order.

Since the dad was starting over furnishing a home, I contributed to the set up in a small way. I brought a handful of used items that I could spare and bought bedding for the boys' bunkbeds. I didn't mind, in fact I was thrilled to help and to be allowed back into Jacob's life, even if he hadn't yet set foot in his soon to be second home. The three of us worked on getting the house ready and when I left, I knew that I was that much closer to seeing Jacob.

CHAPTER 14

The Big Day

THE DAY HAD finally come around the first of October. I was on my way to visit Jacob for the first time in three and half years. Learning that ribs were his favorite, I stopped off to pick up spareribs at the Newport Rib Company and then navigated the 55 free-way during the weekday 5 o'clock traffic. I could hardly contain myself, I was going to be reunited with a now eight year old Jacob after three plus years of no contact. Would he remember me? Obviously I would have no trouble recognizing him, since I had been seeing him every few months from a distance. And because of this I felt a calmness that I otherwise wouldn't have had if I hadn't seen him at all.

It took about an hour to drive the eighteen miles and when I pulled up in front of the house—driving the same black BMW that he hopefully would recognize—I said a silent prayer before I got out of my car.

Jacob hadn't been told that I was coming over; he was running around with three other neighborhood boys, laughing and having fun. After I parked my car at the curb, and got out, I took a minute to stand there and take in the moment. In that instant, I saw Jacob and only Jacob glance over at me. We held eye contract for maybe three seconds. I thought it was interesting that none of the other boys noticed me arrive. There's no denying that instant connection, if even for brief seconds. I don't know if he recognized the black car first, or me? It didn't matter, he knew me and that's all that counts.

Jacob's dad was sitting outside watching the kids, along with his stepdad, and after a few minutes, he called Jacob over. That's when I handed over my video camera so the dad could document the moment. And then I bent down and said to Jacob, "Hi Jacob, I'm Grandma Susan. Do you remember me?"

He was shy and maybe a little uncomfortable with the other boys around, but he nodded smiling and said, " Oh yeah you used to bring me toys and play with me."

I said, "That's right, like street hockey and games." The greeting was short, and I gave him a hug and told him to go back and play.

I joined the men sitting on the front porch where I finally began to breathe again. Sure I had seen him about three months prior at the beach, but I couldn't let on that I wasn't surprised by how he had grown and changed. Seeing him from a distance may have lessened the anxiety but not the excitement or the joy that a reciprocal relationship would bring.

I couldn't take my eyes off him and kept the video camera running as a way to commemorate the occasion. When it was time to go in for dinner, it was just Jacob and his little five year-old brother and me in the kitchen.

I helped get the food on the table, and then the two boys and I ate together while the dad was busy in the garage. Jacob ate his ribs with hardly any conversation, while his brother was a little chatterbox until his dad came in the room and urged him to stop talking and start eating. He didn't, so I began to feed him. He seemed to want my attention, which was hard because then it drew my focus away from Jacob. That all changed when the other grandma, the dad's mom walked in the door. The little brother's response, "you're here again?" She laughed and began cleaning up the kitchen and mumbling something about wanting to tuck him into bed.

I used the distraction as a way to make my exit so that I could join Jacob, who now was sitting on the floor in the living room watching TV. I entered the room about the same time that he was told to go do his homework. The dad added, "Maybe Grandma Susan, wants to help?" I jumped in, "Sure, I'd love to."

Jacob and I went to his room and sat on the floor together and worked on spelling. Then I quizzed him on the list of words. When we finished, I pulled out a photo album that I had brought along to help jog his memory of the two us together since he was a baby. That and the alone time in his room seemed to break the ice. By the end of the evening when I was about to leave, we were best pals. I hugged him and told him I loved him when I tucked him into bed and said good-night. His dad took a picture of that moment that I would not only cherish but use on the cover of my second book.

I was on top of the world as I drove home and best of all no more clandestine episodes. My dream had come true.

Two weeks later I visited again and when I walked in the little brother came running from the bathroom fresh from the tub, arms outstretched and soaking wet, yelling at the top of his lungs, "Gra..a… a… a…ndma Susan!" He jumped into my arms so fast we both nearly toppled to the floor.

I looked at Jacob who was sitting on a recliner scowling. Once I detached myself from the brother and sat him next to me on the sofa, I began talking to Jacob.

He was cool and distant and when I asked his dad about it, he explained that Jacob's mother had gotten angry when she learned that I had been there. Not only had *he* gotten an earful, but Jacob had as well. He confided that she had told Jacob that I wasn't his real grandma, instead saying I was a fake grandma.

Thinking of something we could do together, I had brought along an extra drawing tablet and set of colored pencils so that Jacob and I could draw together during our visit. It took a while but after twenty minutes or so, he joined me on the sofa to watch me draw. It wasn't long after that that the two us were sitting side by side drawing together. When his dad reminded him that they had to get going soon, Jacob, turned his head toward me, and said, "Aw, do you have to leave, can't we draw longer?"

Even though the visit had gotten off to a rocky start, the time spent was quality.

I was seeing more and more of Jacob and I was even asked to babysit a couple of times at seven o'clock on Saturday mornings so that the dad could go to work. I was thrilled. I made the boys pancakes and bacon, cleaned up the kitchen and even did some laundry. It was too risky to take them out in my car in case of an accident, so we played games and rode bikes outside.

The next visit had caused even more duress with Jacob's mom than the previous ones because it was the first time that I took him out of the house alone. We went to Norms restaurant where Jacob enjoyed a plate of chocolate chip pancakes. He was subdued again until his tummy was full and I gave him money to win a stuffed toy from the glass cage near the entrance.

We had been gone about an hour and by the time we arrived back at his house he was happy and chatty. As soon as we walked in, he was directed to the bathroom to take his shower before bed. Jacob, hugged me and kissed me goodbye and as he headed into the bathroom, he shouted over his shoulder, "Dad make sure you don't tell that we went to Norms." He was referring to his little brother who had been taken to his grandma's house to avoid him blabbing about our outing.

Nothing was easy during these turbulent times created by a contentious divorce. Every day it was something. Jacob had been pressured into confessing about the car ride and the dinner date at Norms. What was supposed to be a simple dinner ended up becoming a major event. The dad was beside himself from the constant pressure, even saying, "Now I understand why your son gave up." That's when he asked me if I knew any nice single women. I felt bad for him and introduced him to my hairdresser. The two of them hit it off right away and next thing I knew we were all enjoying a day at Victoria Beach just steps away from my house in Laguna Beach. The hairdresser had a son a year older than Jacob and all three kids had a blast digging to China in the sand.

That was a Sunday and come Monday night I got a call from Jacob's mother wanting all of the details. Being drawn into their battle by peppering me with questions put me on the spot and made for an uncomfortable conversation. They were separated and were no longer accountable to one another about how they spent their free time, yet the interrogation continued.

Jacob's mom wanted me to back off from seeing him until after the divorce was final, citing the reason was the potential unnecessary stress that would add to their already contentious situation. As a way to extend an olive branch and hopefully come to an amicable solution, I suggested a meet up at a coffee shop in Orange. We met but nothing came of it in the way of a compromise, the demand was the same, stop seeing Jacob. I didn't.

CHAPTER 15

The Divorce

JACOB'S PARENT'S DIVORCE grew more and more combative, and the fact that I was now seeing Jacob placed me as a party to the case.

The closest I got to celebrating Thanksgiving with Jacob was a Sunday dinner where ham and mashed potatoes was served at the other grandma's house. A couple of weeks later was Jacob's school holiday program, which his dad had originally invited me to attend, but then there was silence. The day of the event I had made numerous attempts to contact the dad about directions, parking and seating and when I didn't get a call back, I went on my own. The program had been scheduled over two nights, and it was known that the mom and her family had attended the night before, so I didn't have to worry about that problem.

When I entered the church, I spotted the dad, his mother, her husband and Jacob's little brother. As I approached them, everyone looked surprised to see me. As luck would have it there was an empty seat next to the group and as soon as I sat down, little brother jumped from the other grandma's lap to mine. At least one person was happy to see me. It was a struggle with my video camera to try to film the event with the child squirming on my lap until his grandmother convinced him to go back to his seat.

In the end, I was so happy to be able to see Jacob perform and to have recorded the moment. It was important that he knew that I was there for him and supported his efforts. Children's Christmas programs always brought tears to my eyes. This night was no different.

As we filed out of the church, the dad pulled me aside and informed me that I shouldn't let Jacob see me. I didn't know what to say? He explained that his attorney had suggested I stay away until they go to court. He promised to tell Jacob that I had been there and the reasons why I wasn't allowed to interact with him. It was a blow and I cried all the way home. Looking on the bright side, I did get to go to the performance and I did have my video record to comfort me. The thing is, kids love it when family members attend their activities, and then heap the praise, they so richly deserve for accomplishments, upon them.

A few days before Christmas, Jacob's dad relented and decided that it would be OK for me to deliver a Tony Hawk skate board for him and action figure toys for his brother.

And then to my delight when Christmas Eve rolled around, I was included in the holiday celebration after all. It was an informal affair that included games and a buffet at the dad's parents' house. My hairdresser, now the dad's steady girlfriend came along with her son, who was now Jacob's good buddy. This was the first time that I had shared a holiday with Jacob that was actually on the holiday.

Not long after the first of the year my visits became even more restricted. There were a number of legal hurdles to jump through as it was and bringing Jacob's biological grandmother into the mix only added to the list. The judge verbally ordered a temporary stay away order to the parents until further motion of the court.

Even though I had the benefit of an experienced family law attorney with extensive background in grandparent cases to consult with there wasn't much that I could do legally. I did not have standing because of the language of the current laws prohibiting grandparents from filing for visitation following a stepparent adoption.

The dad was kind enough to keep in touch and, once, his girlfriend arranged for me to see Jacob from atop a bluff where he was fishing in a pond at a park in Laguna Niguel. He had informed me that there was a delay in the divorce because Jacob's mom wanted a written agreement signed by both parents to keep me away permanently. He promised that he would never sign the letter that she wanted stipulated in the divorce decree.

The New Year had gotten off to a pretty bad start now that my visits had been placed on hold.

Now, more motivated than ever, it was time to take action and re-visit the legislative arena. In January of 2006 I walked into California State Assemblyman Van Tran's office in Costa Mesa. It was Assemblyman Tran's second year as a member of the California legislature replacing Ken Maddox, with whom I had met previously and who had denied authoring a grandparent bill. I was greeted by the office manager, a pretty blond woman, Trish Klawon, also a grandmother. A few minutes later, the Assemblyman entered the waiting room and looked around for a grandmother. When I stepped forward and reached out to shake his hand, he said, "You're the grandmother?"

I laughed and nodded. Looking embarrassed, he replied, "I was expecting someone older." The stereotypical image we've all seen in the storybooks was most likely his reference. An aside, we've had grandparents in their 30's attend our support group.

The meeting was less than 30 minutes. Referencing my own personal experience, I cited the negative consequences that affected my grandson and myself as a result of becoming victims of the existing California law. There was a huge gap in the law that prevented grandparents from continuing the relationship with grandchildren following a stepparent adoption.

He listened intently, rose from his chair, and said, "I'll carry your bill."

Just like that he agreed, no hesitation, no, "I'll get back to you." I couldn't believe it. And technically I wasn't even a constituent.

My promise to him was that I would become actively involved and do whatever he needed to make sure that the bill passed and became law on the first try. Little did I know that I had my work cut out for me. I had quit my job earlier so I could devote all of my attention to getting legislation passed.

Four months later in May, I flew back to Sacramento, this time my presence welcome, to testify on behalf of the bill during the Judiciary Committee hearing. The day before I was to leave, I was notified that testimony wasn't necessary because the bill would be added to the Consent Calendar. This was a good thing since it was a non-controversial bill and had no fiscal impact. Assemblyman Tran's office explained that I should plan on coming up anyway as an observer of the session and then as a sponsor/lobbyist for the bill. It was an exciting experience to watch the committee meeting and then afterward to deliver a proposal letter, drafted by Tran's office, to the remaining legislators. I walked up and down the halls entering as many offices as I could in one afternoon. I mostly met with staff, however a few of the actual Assembly members did take the time to talk to me.

My lobbying efforts continued after I returned home. I wrote letters to everyone I could think of and various organizations, including the big one, AARP. The purpose of the correspondence was an appeal for support on behalf of the bill.

I spent hours on the phone and in Assemblyman Tran's office faxing updated support correspondence to the Senate Judiciary Committee and all legislators. It was important to keep the bill alive by consistently keeping it in the forefront.

CHAPTER 16

The Last Visit

FATHER'S DAY JUNE 17, 2006 was the last day that I spent with Jacob. It had been five months since the judge had suggested no visitation until the next court appearance, whenever that was going to happen. My attorney agreed that I should be able to see Jacob since I wasn't a party to the case and there was not a restraining order placed specifically on me by the judge. Jacob's dad was reluctant, but acquiesced since it was Father's Day and they were spending it at a public place. I met Jacob, his brother, dad and his parents at the 15th street beach on the Newport Beach peninsula. I did my best to hide my tears when I saw Jacob. It was such a delight to spend time with him again, but I didn't want to alarm him by crying. I stayed close by during the nearly three hours we were at the beach. We spent most of the time at the water's edge collecting shells. When the tide flowed ashore with a new batch, I would trap as many as I could under my toes. As the tide ebbed, Jacob and I quickly collected the treasures and placed them into the pail that I was in charge of holding. This went on for nearly two hours until he was summoned to the beach towel to eat his sandwich.

As Jacob headed back to his family, he turned and motioned with his hand for me to join them. I walked back up to the dry sand and sat next to Jacob where I was offered an egg salad sandwich, which I declined. Instead of eating I used the opportunity to snap some photos of him eating and then posing with his brother. Before Jacob and I returned to the water's edge, I asked his grandpa to shoot some video of the two us. The time together went by quickly. The day had been bittersweet, being with him had been great but I couldn't help but have a sad feeling inside my heart as we walked toward our cars. We were saying our good-byes in front of the Catholic Church on Balboa Boulevard and when I bent down to hug him and kiss him, I knew it would be the last time. I can still feel his little soft white tee shirt beneath my hand as I pressed it against his little back.

There was indeed fallout from that little Father's Day interaction. Everyone got in trouble and that was the end of the visits until the next divorce court hearing.

Due to the circumstances, I wouldn't be celebrating Jacob's birthday in July so I had my daughter deliver the present a few weeks later. I parked down the street from the dad's house while Courtney delivered the skimboard that I had gotten for him. I handed her my small camera and asked her to take some photos for me. She took her dog, Diamond, who ended up being part of the photos. What was important was that Jacob knew the gift was from me and that through no fault of mine was I not seeing him.

The lobbying effort kept my mind occupied and off the unrelenting pain that I lived with daily. If even temporarily. As the sponsor of my bill, the lobbying consumed the better part of the year, from the beginning of 2006 lasting seven months. Ensuring that the bill passed was my full time job now along with running a non-profit. I realized that quitting my job at the golf course had been the right decision.

Assemblyman Tran's Costa Mesa office continued to provide a workspace for me to borrow. Now, with a second round of follow up after the bill crossed over to the senate, there was more faxing and copying bill information to send to all 120 legislators. Once again, I walked the halls of Sacramento to lend my services. I made telephone calls, sent last minute letters and emails as a follow-up and also to new influential organizations and individuals as an effort to build additional support.

As a result of hard work by everyone connected to the effort, the bill passed. In August of 2006, Assemblyman Tran personally called me at home on the night that Governor Schwarzenegger signed the bill. The bill had passed unanimously with all 120 legislators voting for its passage. He was as proud of the accomplishment as I was.

The bill was signed into law January 2007: California family code 3104 (b) (5), which states that grandparents may file a petition for visitation if the child has been adopted by a stepparent.

Shortly after the passage, Assemblyman Van Tran held a celebration party in his office that was attended by his staff, along with my mother, aunt, uncle, and friends. Even Jacob's adoptive dad came to lend support.

The following month in February of 2007, the court date finalizing Jacob's parents' divorce was finally scheduled after year and a half.

When I didn't hear back from the dad about the judges ruling on my visits, I called him and he said they were still working things out and would call me back the next day.

Something didn't sound right. I had a bad feeling about him signing the stay-away letter. When I didn't hear back from him, I drove to the clerk's office of the court in Orange where I was directed to an adjacent room that held a bank of computer terminals for public use. I logged onto their computers where I was able to locate the dissolution document after providing pertinent information. I didn't want to look it over in that room, so I paid the clerk for the printed document and left the crowded office. There was an unoccupied bench in the hall where I seated myself and began reading the divorce case file. On page 8 of 10 under—Child Custody—miscellaneous was my name.

It read:

Re-Susan Hoffman

Jacob's biological grandmother, Susan Hoffman, will continue to be restrained from contact with Jacob unless otherwise agreed to in writing by both parties.

It went on to spell out the details. I was not allowed within a 100 feet, I was not allowed to send emails, cards, letters, or gifts, and no 3rd party communication—signed by both parents.

I was actually written into their divorce decree! I sat on that bench reading it over and over, not caring who saw me crying.

Following the passage of my law that now gave a grandparent standing following a stepparent adoption, which was my situation, and the fact that I was now permanently restrained from visiting Jacob, I hired the attorney who was an expert in grandparent cases and who had advised me to change the law. She drafted the petition for visitation using my own law and I actually hand carried it to the clerk of the court so I could file it myself.

On the day of the hearing, the judge wasn't even aware of the new law nor was the opposing counsel. My attorney had to educate them. The judge was unreasonable and ultimately violated my civil rights by not providing me the opportunity to be heard. Her reasoning in denying my petition was because she wanted to see a change of circumstance between the parents' case. The dad had come forward at this point and tried to withdraw his signature from the previous agreement by including a letter of support of my visitation in the petition. Since he had originally gone along with the mother's demand to sign a letter of agreement to keep me away, the judge refused to allow my petition and also to hear the dad's support declaration. He stood up during the court hearing and faced the judge trying to undo what he had previously signed but the judge shook her head and denied his testimony.

She repeated a few times, citing the change of circumstance criteria as the only option to revisit the case. No amount of pleading from my attorney would sway the judge's opinion.

I was devastated when we left the courtroom. A few days later my attorney and her assistant invited me to lunch to discuss the situation. By now we had become friends. Her advice was to let it go and enjoy my life.

CHAPTER 17

The Grand Wishes

I WENT HOME to my new place in Corona del Mar, and started writing. I wrote all day everyday. It was therapeutic. It gave me purpose. It kept me sane. One of my grandparent clients from the group referred her cousin, Marchelle Hammack who had a literary background, to become my editor. My book was titled *Grand Wishes*, which was about grandparent visitation issues, beginning with my situation, something I knew a lot about. I included story contributions from grandparent clients, chapters about the legislative process and starting a non-profit organization. Writing was cathartic and helped me get through losing Jacob a second time. The grandparents in my support group were an important source of comfort as well. It truly became a reciprocal arrangement. To be able to sit in a room with people who understand because they share the experience makes a huge difference in dealing with grief.

And, the reason that I started a support group to begin with, I wanted someone to talk to.

The other change in my life was to move again. I had made a mistake when I bought my condo in Corona del Mar because I bought it for the wrong reasons. I thought if I had a larger nicer home that Jacob would want to come and visit since I would have a room for him, whereas my Laguna Beach cottage was pretty rustic and only had one bedroom.

The Corona Del Mar home was more space than I needed and far exceeded my means. I sold it at a loss, but I didn't care I just wanted to get out. I hated the neighborhood, which was noisy and disruptive to my writing as well quiet enjoyment.

I found a modest home in a mobile home park for a fraction of the price and with a water view of the back-bay. As soon as I got settled in, I picked up my writing again. This time the neighborhood was quiet, people respectful and the view of the water created a sense of peace and tranquility.

When Christmas rolled around, a new idea sprouted. I discovered the charitable organization, World Vision, where one could donate a goat, or chicken or just about any farm animal to feed a third world family and the best part was that the acknowledgment would be sent anonymously to anyone of my choosing. I bought the goat and had the thank you letter sent to Jacob. It felt good.

I wrote every day until I completed the book in the fall of 2007 and then taught myself how to self-publish, which included hiring a book formatter, cover designer, and professional book printer. It was a time consuming, humbling experience and unexplored territory for me.

Self-marketing was a challenge, and probably the most frustrating part of the process. Maybe it was the subject that opened doors, but to my delight, my first book signing at Barnes and Noble in Aliso Viejo, September 2008 was well attended by friends and family and by grandparents who had found me through the organization, including a couple from Seattle. It was an exciting time.

At the request of the Seattle couple, who had driven from Washington state to attend my book signing, I flew to Seattle for a January 3rd book signing at the Barnes and Noble Northgate location. The Seattle grandparents had formed their own support group with about 20 of them in attendance. They had many questions and it was a lively presentation. From there I went to Spokane and did a much smaller signing at another Barnes and Noble.

There was another signing at the Costa Mesa Borders bookstore and a news piece with an interview for the Time Warner cable channel.

CHAPTER 18

The Recommencement of Detecting

IT WAS BACK to the job of reconnaissance. Since Jacob now knew who I was, I had to be careful about getting too close, especially during a field trip. I didn't want to put him in an awkward position nor risk having him telling someone.

Instead I searched for photos of him online through his school and parents' Facebook pages.

Now that he was in seventh grade, there were fewer field trips. Then during one of my school searches I discovered an upcoming field trip that was a tour of downtown Los Angeles scheduled for May. The itinerary provided a pretty detailed timeline of the walking tour which helped me plan my observation point.

The blond wig was back on my head and once again part of my undercover attire. It was now going on three years since Jacob, now eleven, had seen me. This time my surveillance would be a family affair. I brought my daughter Courtney along and we met my cousin Gif, who lived in Los Angeles, at a designated downtown spot. My thinking was that it would be less conspicuous and we would blend in better if the three of us were having lunch about the same time Jacob and his school was there.

We sat at an outdoor table in the Wells Fargo Plaza, which was located on Grand Avenue in downtown Los Angeles. I had my big camera, so I got up and nonchalantly moseyed over to where Jacob's class was roaming around and I pretended to take pictures of the building. I managed to click off a couple of photos before a burly security guard of around 60, toting a gun and dressed in a gray uniform approached and informed me that cameras were not allowed in the area. I was stunned. When I asked why, he said it had to do with bank security. I tried not to show my embarrassment as I casually strolled back toward my family. That's all I needed—to get busted in front Jacob and his classmates. Hopefully no one noticed. It was clearly evident that I was upset when I sat down with my daughter and cousin. I had come all this way and now I couldn't take photos of Jacob. A few minutes later, my cousin asked which one was Jacob and then when the guard had his back turned he took a few quick photos with his cell phone as he pretended to be talking. Being close to him and watching him interact with the other kids was satisfaction enough, although having a photo always made the experience last longer.

Withe the field trips few and far between, my frustration was growing about the lack of opportunities to see him now that he was older. It had been almost one year since I had last seen Jacob during the Los Angeles field trip.

Since everything fell apart after my petition for visitation court case, I had no more communication with the dad or any of his family. I contacted the private investigator again and that's when it was confirmed that Jacob had moved to Aliso Viejo.

I wondered about that after I had driven by the house once and saw different cars and people which, is how I learned that the family no longer lived in the same house. It then took him several surveillance tries to figure out which school Jacob was attending now that he was in eighth grade. Once I learned which school, I set out once again to find him.

Jacob was now in a public middle school and according to the school's website, they didn't have any field trips scheduled. I did, however see something about school photos, so I called the school and was given the name of the company and their phone number so I could arrange to purchase photos. I called them, gave them Jacob's name and supplied a credit card over the phone; about a week later I drove to San Clemente and picked up my order of school photos. I was so happy and so surprised to see how much he had changed as a preteen.

I made several trips to the middle school that he was attending sometimes relying on others for assistance. A few different grandparents from my group offered to drive me in their car so that I wouldn't be spotted in a familiar car by either parent. My next door neighbor, Diana, who was always game for any new adventure offered to accompany me a couple of times. The first time we went was in the late afternoon because I thought maybe Jacob had been in the after school daycare program. We sat in the parking lot where I got a little paranoid and shrank down low so as not to be seen as we watched parents pulling in and out of the parking lot. We didn't see him. Another time, Lana, from the grandparent group drove and again no sighting. Same with Earl, also from the group. Each time we sat in the parking lot and waited for school to let out, and then watched the swarms of kids exiting in all different directions using a variety of walkways. During another trip when Diana went with me, we parked on the street near one of the entrances instead of in the lot. By car we followed a group of boys walking toward a nearby condo complex. I didn't want to get too close, but I was pretty sure Jacob was one of them. I had his portrait photo and I had also seen his picture on Facebook so I had an idea about how much he had grown during the time that I hadn't seen him. From where we were parked, it looked like two of the boys went into one of the condos. I was pretty sure he was one of them. Maybe there was an arrangement for him to go home with a friend until his mom arrived?

I wanted a closer view to make sure, so I went back on my own a few days later and again parked near the same stairs that he had used before and waited for the mass exit. I kept my eyes on the rear view mirror so I would be able to see his face and there he was. I couldn't let it go at that though. I pulled away from the curb and followed the boys as they turned right onto the residential street where I had seen them before. This was tricky being out in the open snooping around in a neighborhood that I had no legitimate reason to visit. It wouldn't have been smart to take any photos under those circumstances; I would just have to tuck the memory away in my head instead.

Clearly there would be no more summer camp with field trips, which meant I would have to wait until he started high school in the fall to see him again.

That June my grandparent group, that was now a full fledged non-profit organization, had our first fundraiser at the OASIS senior center. To me it was a success with over 120 people in attendance. I invited a former state senator, a psychologist and an attorney to speak to the audience. The afternoon affair with desserts and iced tea generated a number of donations from our silent auction and sales from my second book. I hired a cameraman to help me shoot video of the event for a potential documentary film, which would be my next big project.

Because we offer support to everyone, a number of our inquiries come through emails and phone calls. And since we don't always meet each client, the event provided a great opportunity to put a face with the name. When one of the grandparent clients who attended the event happened to mention that she had a friend who worked in the same school district that Jacob was attending a light bulb went on inside my head. Toward the end of summer I contacted her friend about the possibility of me volunteering at Jacob's high school, soon to start in September. The parent volunteer process was a little more complicated than I realized and once she explained the details, like membership in PTA, I decided it wasn't a good fit. But then she hatched a plan that would provide me with Jacob's class schedule, except I would have to wait a month or so until things settled down with the new semester starting.

I grew impatient waiting to get his schedule and looked for another opportunity for a Jacob sighting. I asked Jean, a grandparent from our group to help me. She had been alienated from two of her grandkids, but her step- granddaughter who she was able to see and who was the same age as Jacob, attended the same high school. One day I rode along with her to pick up her granddaughter from school hoping that I would also see Jacob. I was stunned at the enormous amount of kids exiting the school when the bell rang. It was as though a herd of cattle was about to stampede with all of students rushing in one direction. This made it impossible to spot Jacob.

We dropped her granddaughter off and then I asked her to drive by Jacob's house in the off chance that maybe he walked home in which case I could catch a glimpse. The P.I. had given me the address but this was the first time I had driven by. Once again it was located on a cull-de -sac, so that meant a strange car would have drawn attention. We drove around the cross streets to see if we could spot Jacob maybe walking home, which I didn't count on since it was pretty far. As we were making one last loop on the same cross street, I spotted a tall, slender, dark haired boy wearing a headset and walking alone toward the direction we had just come from. I wasn't absolutely sure if it was him, so I asked Jean to make another U—turn so I could get a better look. We cruised by slowly this time and sure enough it was him. We then turned into the street across from his and waited to make sure he made a right turn onto his street. He did, and I screamed with joy. We both started laughing. Mission accomplished. Success.

We headed back to Corona del Mar to the grandparent meeting that I had someone start for me and could hardly wait to share the good news with the group.

About the middle of October, my friend's friend came through with the schedule. I knew that once I had access to his schedule, I would know which direction he was coming from when school let out and that way I could get a better look at him.

As soon as I got his schedule, I located a map of the high school and easily found my way to the computer lab where his last class was. I was a wreck inside, what if I got busted for lurking around the school property? I had no saliva in my mouth and my hands were beginning to tremble. I knew it was important to maintain an aura of confidence, as I kept telling myself, "be calm, act like you belong there." But sitting in front of the classroom on campus was nothing like sitting in the parking lot.

There was a concrete planter wall just outside the room, which is where I parked myself. I brought along a tote bag-as a prop- stuffed with a beach towel sticking out of the top- that I busied myself re-arranging as I waited for the bell to ring. My thinking, if someone inquired why I was sitting there, I could say that my grandson was going to a friend's house after school to swim and I was delivering his stuff.

What seemed like an eternity waiting, the bell rang and the door flew open and now I zeroed in on each kid as they rushed from the classroom. Just when I was about to give up thinking everyone had gone, there he was, and yes he did see me, or at least a woman sitting there. I had the wig and sunglasses on, but it's funny, he was the only one, out of all the kids, who actually glanced over at me. It was a quick look, but I could feel the energy and then he walked alone toward the street. I got up and blended in with a group of kids who had been walking nearby. I walked behind him for as long as I could without being conspicuous and then as he headed toward the street, I made my way toward the parking lot and climbed inside my car, waiting until it was safe to leave the premises.

I was happy to have seen Jacob, if only for a few minutes. I wasn't going to make a habit of hanging around the school, I just wanted to maybe drive by once in a while to see him as he left campus.

CHAPTER 19

The Facebook Request

FACEBOOK IS THE platform for anyone wanting to be in the know about other people's lives. Grandparents included. The social media site can be a valuable resource for grandparents wanting to capture a glimpse into their grandchild's life. And for those who have been alienated, landing on the right page can provide a treasure trove of information. If the child is too young to have their own page, the parents along with family and friends frequently provide the links to the photos and posts about the child. At least the grandparents have a window into their developmental changes and activities.

I tracked the list of friends that were on the parents' pages along with anyone I could think of that was connected which eventually led me to photos and chatter. My friend, Carol, who was much more diligent following Facebook activity, provided another pair of eyes in my pursuit of information.

We learned about some of Jacob's amusements, sporting activities and family excursions. My collection of photos of Jacob, as he got older consisted of printouts obtained from Facebook images.

Several months had gone by since my last Jacob sighting—the day he was walking home from school—when I received a "friend" request on Facebook from Jacob's dad. It had been over four years since we had communicated and now he wanted to connect through Facebook. When I clicked on his page there was another surprise, his home page photo was of him holding Courtney's dog Diamond with both boys on either side. Courtney had taken that photo for me the day she delivered the skimboard five years before, since I couldn't give it to Jacob myself because of the court order.

I sat frozen staring at the computer screen, not knowing what to do. I did finally accept the friend request and then followed up with a private Facebook message. I wanted to know about Jacob.

The "friend" gesture re-opened the door to further communication with the dad. It was important to forgive and move on. We spoke on the phone and he explained that Jacob had been asking about me, and now that he was fifteen a judge would have most likely given him a voice in court. Since neither of us wanted to return to court or subject Jacob to the experience, we knew it would be best to wait.

In the mean time becoming Facebook friends with the dad brought me that much closer to Jacob's world.

CHAPTER 20

The Furtive Visits

LETS JUST SAY that I encountered Jacob as he grew older.

I learned that he played La Crosse for one semester so I attended one of his away games held at Corona Del Mar High School, which was near my home. I stood far away on another field that bordered the perimeter of the school and used my long lens camera to figure out which one was Jacob. Even though he couldn't see me, it was important that I came out to support his efforts. Who knows, maybe he somehow knew I was there…somewhere? I was a little uneasy about being seen, since his mom was there in the bleachers. At one point, I managed to sneak over to a closer location for a better view, using a handball court as a shield.

The next fall Jacob was on the soccer team and again I was incognito when I went to his game. The game was in San Clemente and I had to be careful about being seen. I steered clear of the bleachers and found a spot at the far end of the field where I shot a video of Jacob running back and forth chasing the ball across the field with his teammates.

The reunification began with an email when Jacob sent me a message. It had been over seven years since we had been together that Father's Day at the beach. To go from interacting with a child of eight to a teenager was quite a jump. I had missed being part of all of those growth stages and now I was communicating with a teenager. He wrote, "Hi Susan, this is Jacob."

My response, "Hi Jacob, I can't believe it's really you? So, tell me what have you been doing the last…years?"

To be back in his life, even if it was through email, and for him to know that I hadn't forgotten was huge. And no more chasing posts to find out what he was up to.

The hows, whens and whys no longer mattered, what counted now was that we could begin to build some sort of a connection again and that my grandson would know that I was there for him. Always.

Suddenly he was a senior and high school graduation was coming up. When Jacob and I talked about it, he said that he would reserve a ticket for me. With a limited attendance capacity, each student was given ten tickets. We arranged for me to meet him in a shopping center parking lot near school a few days before graduation was to take place so that I could give him money to buy my ticket. I returned the next day to the same meeting place and he handed me the coveted ticket. He said that he had more than ten family members who wanted to attend, and was scrambling to find extra tickets from other students. I was grateful that he had kept his word.

The four o'clock graduation time turned out to be a very warm June afternoon. As I stood in line to get in to the high school stadium, I could feel the sweat trickling down my back as I kept my eyes peeled for any unwanted confrontations. Once I was admitted with my ticket, I then stepped up to the entrance to the field, where I flashed my press pass and was admitted onto the field so that I could take photos. I had actually arranged with a local news publication to shoot photos at no charge since I was planning on attending the ceremony anyway.

With all the chaos, no one paid any attention to me. I made my way down the center aisle and past the rows of folding chairs for the graduates until I was at the front. From there I walked over to the sidelines and found a shady spot below the bleachers and out of view. I leaned against the concrete wall and breathed a sigh of relief. My big straw hat and loose clothing hid my body and gait that could have been recognized.

When the music began with the graduation march, I instantly stood at attention focusing on the kids making their way toward the field. They were all proceeding forward in one line and then at a certain point were splitting off—some going toward the right and some toward the left. Oh, no! The what-ifs were churning inside my head, having no idea which side Jacob was going to end up on. What if he went left? How would I get to the other side of the field now that the ceremony started without calling attention to myself? I held my breath, waited... waited... and then I saw him...and he did turned right! He was now headed right toward me. Oh thank you, Lord ...click, click, click, my shutter snapped away, and when he saw me, he smiled and gave a brief wave. He was very cool revealing black Converse high top sneakers from beneath the gown, and oh so handsome. After the speeches, row by row, the seniors began to make their way to the stage to accept their diplomas. This was also my cue. I took a deep breath and marched over to the center of the field where the graduating students were seated in front of the stage. I kneeled down and began shooting again, taking close up shots of kids as they received their diplomas. In reality, I only wanted a close up of Jacob as he received his diploma, which I got. But that would have been obvious. I then sat in one of the white folding chairs in the front row amongst the graduates and continued to shoot photos of the remainder of the ceremony. I was stuck at that point and couldn't go running back to my hiding place.

After the hat toss, I tried to give Jacob his gift, but he was running to return his gown and said he'd meet me after. I knew that wasn't going to happen with the beehive of activity and swarm of people funneling out of the stadium. I got pinned between band members toting their instruments, and was carried along with the tide. Once I finally broke through the crowd into an open space, there was a line at the shuttle buses that I had originally ridden from the distant parking lot. I just wanted to get out of there and the idea of standing in line for the bus was not appealing. I looked around for another way. That's when I recognized two men who had participated in the ceremony standing in front of their cars that were parked in a convenient VIP spot. They were chatting away when I boldly approached them and asked if either of them was headed in the direction of the federal building that had been the designated parking lot for the graduation attendees. One of them said he'd be happy to drop me off, so I hopped in his little silver BMW and found out he was actually the mayor of Aliso Viejo and had been one of the speakers at the ceremony. I had been so focused on Jacob that I hadn't paid attention to the names of any of the folks on stage or what they had to say.

When the nice man kindly pulled up behind my car, I thanked him and as I closed the passenger door, I noticed a black car that looked similar to Jacob's, and was parked next to mine. As I moved closer, I stopped dead in my tracks. It *was* Jacob's car and he was sitting in it looking at his phone. He had backed in, which is why he was facing my direction. So when he looked up about the same time I looked at him, both of us were stunned to see the other. Out of all of the thousands of cars how was it possible that I ended up next to the only person that I came to see? The stars were aligned and the gods were smiling down on us. The day just kept getting better. Jacob hopped out of his car, and I gave him a congratulatory hug followed by handing him his gift. We sat in his front seat and he opened the GoPro camera, which was something he wanted. Our accidental visit was ever-so brief, since he was expected at his mother's house to celebrate immediately following graduation. What I had, the one on one, was better than any party! What a day!

CHAPTER 21

The Adult Jacob

I DIDN'T KID myself—with more freedom, came independence and visiting grandma wasn't exactly a priority. I understood, and had no expectations, I was content knowing that he knew that I loved him and wasn't going away. Ever.

There was so much that I wanted to do for Jacob to make up for all of the Christmas and birthday gifts that I wasn't allowed to give him. A shopping spree seemed like a good place to start. We met in front of a surf shop in Laguna Beach. As we stepped through the front door of the shop, I could see his eyes light up at the sight of all of the cool stuff. He took his time browsing while I watched as he carefully considered his choices. He always checked with me before he added to the pile and when he was done, he thanked me more than once. Afterward, we walked to a nearby Mexican restaurant called El something for dinner, where we had a view of the sun about to slip below the horizon behind the beach across the street.

We met once at an Italian restaurant, Ti Amo by Il Barone in South Laguna to commemorate a birthday. Christmas morning was celebrated at Starbucks with a stack of gifts consisting of clothes that he wanted.

Jacob accepted the cloak and dagger, which may have sparked a degree of excitement. No one wanted to upset the applecart, so we kept a low profile for meet-ups and away from little brother who was a conduit of information between both parents.

Jacob turned 18 years old the month after graduation. He was now a legal adult. How did this happen so fast?

He had been working at a local restaurant and planned to enroll in junior college in the fall. Now that he was a young man, and busy with school and work, our visits mostly amounted to special occasions. Our mode of communication was by texting.

A year and a half after graduating, Jacob decided to join the U.S. Coast Guard. He was 19 years old. We created some nice memories before he departed in January.

We had celebrated his 18th birthday at Seasons 52 restaurant in South Coast Plaza, his 19th at Bear Flag in Crystal Cove, a Christmas lunch at Houston's restaurant and finally a few days before he left for boot-camp, we enjoyed a quiet good-bye lunch in my home with take out from Sharkey's Woodfire Mexican Grill in Newport Coast.

Jacob and I stayed in touch by way of text messaging during the three months that he was at boot camp in New Jersey. His cell phone usage was restricted and what calls he made were understandably mostly to his girlfriend back home.

His graduation in March was attended by his girlfriend, his parents, stepparent, grandparents and brother. I wasn't invited and most likely wouldn't have gone if the topic had come up. I figured it would have been a quick turn around with everyone showing up for the brief ceremony. His dad confirmed afterward that there had been too many family members and not enough Jacob to go around.

Seven months later in August of that year, I arranged to visit Jacob who was stationed in Charleston South Carolina.

I have always wanted to visit the South and now I had the opportunity to combine a road trip as part of my journey. With Diamond, now my dog, I flew to Houston rented a car the next day and set out for a three-day road trip to Charleston. Texas was big and took forever to cross into Louisiana. We arrived to a rainy New Orleans during peak five o'clock traffic and got lost.

The next day was more enjoyable, spending time in Biloxi Mississippi. A fan of the author, John Grisham, I had always wanted to visit his hometown that he lovingly describes in his books.

The Chamber of Commerce was located in a grand old southern mansion that was pet friendly. Across the street, there was a lighthouse sitting on the median that divided the roadway in front of the beach. I left the car in the Chamber lot and Diamond and I set off for a nice walk toward the beach. There were Adirondack chairs sitting on the sand and people swimming in the water. Still drizzling, the day had a thick, gray cloud cover that stretched to the ocean, blending with the horizon so you couldn't distinguish where the water ended and the sky began. It was a calm before the storm I suppose and quite lovely. From there I headed toward Columbus Georgia. I got lost in Alabama and didn't check into the Microtel in Columbus, near Fort Lee until nightfall. I have no idea how I eventually found the place. It was the most disgusting lodging I've ever experienced. The room was filthy and smelled like pot. I had booked places that were pet friendly, so it was always slim pickings.

The next day I drove straight through to Charleston South Carolina without incident. The sun was shining and it was hot and humid when we arrived at our vacation home rental, which lived up to the photos. It was a well maintained old cottage that had a porch—like most houses I discovered—with two rocking chairs. The kitchen had all of the amenities, even food. The bed was comfortable, bathroom clean and well appointed overall. On our walks around the neighborhood I noticed the homes were eclectic, ramshackle mixed with well-maintained and the people who lived there, racially diverse.

Jacob was stationed nearby at the Coast Guard base, but he lived out of town in military housing on another base. He came to the rental the next day, on his day off and then played tour guide and showed me around the area. We went out to lunch, left Diamond in the car and then took her to the beach a few miles away. The next day was lunch and Best Buy to pick up a birthday gift for Jacob.

During my stay, I took a day and drove up north to Pawley's Island to visit a grandparent client with whom I had grown close. Carmen and her husband, Jack divided their time between South Carolina and Connecticut and fortunately the timing worked out so I could see them when they were in South Carolina. We had met when I traveled to Hartford Connecticut in 2009 at the request of Carmen and her group. The grandparent group contacted me after reading my book and asked me to help with grandparent legislation by testifying at a focus group led by one of the senate representatives.

The best part of the experience was meeting the four women and gaining some insight about another state's legislative system. The senator chairwoman was an outspoken, feisty, gray-haired woman and one of the first things out of her mouth was, "How'd you ever get someone from California to come here?"

Jacob came home for a visit three months later in November and I managed to see him at his dad's house for a casual dinner a couple of days before his leave ended.

The following year Jacob got another leave to come home in July. I offered him my airplane voucher as a birthday present, which covered most of his flight from South Carolina to California. Now that he was 21, he couldn't wait to go to Las Vegas with his friends from High School. As it turned out, his two- week visit was booked solid and I never got to see him. I tried not to take it personal or let it get me down as I remembered what it was like to be that age.

Six months later in March, Jacob received another leave before he was transferred to Virginia to attend school for intelligence training. The day before we were to get together, he received orders from the Coast Guard to cut the trip short so he could leave for school in Virginia. It had now been a year and four months since I had seen him.

Once he completed his three-month school program, he received a transfer to work in Colorado. That was June and in September I visited him.

Diamond and I lucked out again with our accommodations. The tree-lined neighborhood, just outside Denver, consisted of well-maintained custom homes, large and small. It was conveniently located to shopping and felt very safe. This house was even better than the one in Charleston, with a beautiful large back yard for Diamond, and all of the amenities anyone could want.

Since I didn't have a car, because of the fiasco at the airport car rental lot, I took the Lyft everywhere, except to the market, where I could walk. I went to see Jacob the next day at his new apartment about 20 miles away. This was the first place that he'd had on his own and now shared with his girlfriend. We caught up for a bit before heading out to lunch at a restaurant down the street. When we returned we took Diamond for a walk around the newly built complex that showcased an Olympic sized pool with a swim up bar and molded floating lounges.

The next day, I visited another grandparent client, who had been a long time member of our support group in Newport Beach and who had recently moved to Aurora, Colorado.

Her situation was a sad one. Judy's daughter had been killed by a drunk driver nearly ten years before and the daughter's ex-husband took the two children to Washington state, thereby cutting off all family. Judy found the group shortly after the children had been moved. The connection with other grandparents suffering from alienation provided the support and understanding she needed and helped her process the additional grief.

Judy and her husband, Roy were still getting acclimated to the Colorado lifestyle after living in Southern California for most of their adult lives. They had moved to a 55 and over newly built community with beautiful brand new homes and a gazillion activities. It was fun to see her new environment and, I was hopeful this wouldn't be the only visit. With Jacob stationed in Colorado for at least three years, my plans were to visit at least once a year.

Since I will do whatever it takes to remain in Jacob's life, I will go wherever he is to see him.

CHAPTER 22

The Interpretation

WHEN A LOVING grandparent is removed from a child's life it is harmful for the grandchild and heartbreaking for the grandparent. When parent-grandparent alienation arises, it is painful for all and rips apart the fabric of the family. This punishment of being denied access to a grandchild, which often leaves no room for change, forgiveness or restitution, is a harsh outcome for the grandparents. Arbitrary parental decisions are heartless and cruel when depriving a child of the close contact with a grandparent with whom they have developed a close bond.

While children have no voice and no choice, grandparents do.

There is no right or wrong way to feel when grandparents lose access to a grandchild. Grandparents have to do what they need to do to cope when they become separated from a child, with whom they have established a bond, as a result of parental authority. Their emotional and physical well-being is at risk.

As a grandparent support organization working with disenfranchised grandparents, we have determined that the cause of estrangement comes in many forms. Divorce and separation are the most common scenarios that provide a pathway to bringing in a non-biological third party relationship into the mix.

People not wanting to be alone, including moms and dads often jump into new relationships right off the bat. Therefore, it is the non-biological third party addition into the family that is the most common source of the problem. In other words when the parents are no longer together as a result of divorce, separation or death and the custodial parent then enters into a new relationship, it's the grandparents who often get the boot. The green monster rears its ugly head and the new partner most often does not want a reminder of a previous relationship around.

There was a time when I thought it was rare when death was the cause of grandparents being cutoff from a grandchild, but it's not. Repeatedly there are stories of the surviving spouse alienating the parent of the parent who died. Most often it's a result of a new relationship, but there have been some who simply don't want reminders of the deceased parent. Or the surviving spouse uses the opportunity to terminate a previously tense relationship with the in-laws.

The intact family situation is not an entirely uncommon scenario, just not as widespread as the broken family relationships when it comes to cutting off the grandparents.

The multitude of emotions and a variety of behaviors that I experienced when I became estranged from my grandson, are not unique to me. There is not a specific list or an order to these shared emotions. Once the dust settles it's how one ends up coping with the pain that matters.

Sadness, depression, despair, anger, are all emotional reactions that are best expressed and not repressed. Let it out, experience them. Cry until you can't cry anymore, curl up in the fetal position and sob. Stay in bed, watch TV, read, sleep, stare at the ceiling. Punch something, preferably a punching bag at the gym. Talk therapy with a professional counselor, or folk therapy with a friend, family, or group—all good ways to get it out. And then move on. Getting stuck is self-destructive and affects our ability to overcome the distress and get on with life. Losing access to a beloved grandchild feels like a death but there is life after death, only in some ways the loss is worse because there is no finality. They are out there somewhere but out of reach.

Assuming the emotions that incapacitate us are behind us, devising a plan of action is a likely next step. Some grandparents contact the parents in an effort to make amends. They beg, they plead, they apologize, suggest mediation, therapy. Sometimes they have success and when they don't they jump into court if they have standing and petition for visitation or custody. Once again some receive court ordered visitation, while others fail. It's in the hands of the judges, who have the control. Some grandparents offer money, which parents usually accept, with no guarantees. There are also grandparents who find themselves in situations where they are obligated to continue making payments in exchange for access to a grandkid.

Some grandparents choose to give up and wait until the grandkids are eighteen to see them. They think that the kid is going to come looking for them. Typically this does not happen. It's the grandparents who end up doing the finding. By the time the grandchild reaches eighteen years of age, they have forgotten the grandparents if there hasn't been any communication since they were children. Or even if there has been since they were adolescents, they often don't seek out the grandparent. These are young adults, they have other things on their minds, and looking for grandma and grandpa isn't one of them. They're in college, working, socializing, they are busy, period. Another form of giving up are the grandparents, who choose not to go looking for the grandchild when they turn eighteen. They are afraid of rejection as a result of grandparent alienation produced by parental influence and sometimes brainwashing. Many of these grandparents have moved on with their lives and want to protect themselves from enduring the pain all over again.

Finally, seeing the grandchild grow up by experiencing each year, was not only important to me but may have been to others as well. This is something that, understandably hasn't been shared by those of us who have led a clandestine life in order to see our grandkids from afar, so it's hard to know how prevalent it is.

For me there was no hesitation, I would have done anything to see Jacob each and every year, whether he saw me or not. I can't imagine not seeing him or knowing that he was all right for all those years. It gave me comfort to know that he was a fine growing boy. To be able to watch him play, laugh, interact with other kids helped get me through the suffering. It was still a relationship, just of a different kind. During those years when we were apart, he never knew that I hadn't given up on him, or that I was there watching. But he knows now, and that's better than him thinking I simply walked away and gave up.

A lot of grandparents save the cards and gifts that they will someday give to the kids when they are eighteen, which is a way to provide evidence that they didn't forget. While I did that too, I took it a step further. Not all grandparents have the desire to make that kind of a commitment, it's scary as hell, and I get that. They say it's too painful to see them. True it is painful to see them but more painful not to. Even though they are deprived of knowing you are there, I'd rather endure the pain and know that they were ok and happy, than wonder.

CHAPTER 23

The Coping Strategies

LOSING CONTROL CREATES helplessness and distress, so by doing something rather than nothing relieves some of that tension. Part of doing is changing behavior that is not helping us but hindering us.

LET GO OF THE ANGER: as they say, holding onto anger is like drinking poison and hoping the other person will die. I just know that spending time ticking off all the adverse circumstances and dwelling on the casualties wasn't going to make me feel better. It was only going to drag me down. Part of letting it go was to practice putting myself in the parent's shoes. By doing that, I came up with my own assessment of the "why."

I decided that some individuals don't have the capacity to behave any differently. During conflict, these people get rid of the person instead of the problem. This is who they are, their character, and they're not going to change. It would be like expecting someone with two left feet to perform ballet and once I put it in that perspective it helped me better understand the behavior.

FORGIVENESS FOR YOURSELF: not necessarily for the other person. It wasn't necessary for me to have a face to face or phone call with the parent in order to forgive. It wasn't about them but about me. By forgiving the other person, it brings peace to oneself and lifts the burden, similar to anger. I said those words to myself and released the pretend balloon into the atmosphere.

JOURNALING: write down your thoughts, good and bad. Write to your grandchild. Write to the parents, and if you write negativity, don't mail it. It's a good way of letting off steam in a healthy way. In the beginning, when I was full of anger, I did write the hostile letter, filled with expletives, shaming, blaming and disdain. It felt good and only took one time to vent my anger.

Routinely writing to my grandson was much more fun and fulfilling, and brought him close to me in a way whenever I expressed my thoughts and shared something about my daily life. Some days my correspondence was as simple as jotting down what I did that day. Those little daily reports made me feel as though I was talking to Jacob.

EXERCISE: was my saving grace. If I hadn't had that outlet, I would have gone bonkers. And when I felt at my lowest, that's when I made myself go. I showed up for class and left my troubles at the door. I was better for it, and my workouts made the difference between feeling energized as opposed to spiritless. Exercise being the key to mental and physical well-being can be a life preserver during stressful situations. Exercise gained even more importance in my life after I lost access to Jacob. I desperately needed an outlet and running helped, then I took Pilates, spin classes, body sculpt, yoga and when I wasn't taking a class, I hiked the hills in Laguna Beach, swam laps at the high school pool, rode my bike and walked along the beach. All were invaluable for a healthier mind and body. In the end the most beneficial endeavor was the group classes. They kept me engaged with others and focused because of the consistency. If I signed up, I showed up! Knowing that someone was waiting for me made me accountable. There were days when I was in a funk, but I drug myself to the gym and always felt better after than I did when I got there.

COUNSELING: as for counseling, I lucked out, without wasting time and money with the wrong person. My therapist was a good match. That doesn't always happen, but I can say without a doubt that Rick Harrison was a blessing.

Rick's specialty was in communication skill building. He possessed a knack for teaching the techniques that are required to better get along with difficult people. No job was too big for him, his toolbox was endless.

Talk therapy is an effective coping strategy and even more so when skill building tips are included. The number one tip and basis for everything else: Instead of waiting around for the other person to change, you have to be the one to make the changes.

SOCIAL RELATIONSHIPS: are important in every aspect of life and more so when we're down. I'm not talking about dumping our problems on others, but remaining engaged with others. Participating in activities or community functions, or just greeting others outside our homes whether we know them or not, in other words, some sort of human contact. A smile goes a long way and is contagious. VOLUNTEER: I thought if volunteered with kids it would maybe replace the emptiness of not being able to enjoy the role of grandmother. I couldn't have been more wrong. While it did provide some temporary relief from the distress, eventually it made it worse.

I genuinely wanted to make a difference in a child's life, so I signed up to volunteer at a well-known national children's advocacy program that included foster homes. Once I passed the background check and was fingerprinted, I was assigned to one of the homes in Costa Mesa for training. What I observed was an eye-opener. There was very little structure, the food was inferior and far from nutritious. The workers in the home threw together boxed macaroni and cheese, hamburger helper and basically anything cheap and easy with no attention to health benefits.

What stunned me the most was the attitude of the caregivers assigned to the house. They weren't engaged, or even compassionate but more robot-like going through the motions.

Taking a child away from the house for outings during my scheduled visits was part of the positive experience, until the agreement stopped being honored by the staff. Spending time with a caring adult on a one on one basis was beneficial to the welfare of a child and rewarding for me to make a difference. Taking one of the boys to the jetty to climb on rocks on the Balboa peninsula and the little girl to the beach to dig in the sand was fun. But if there were no guarantees that my time slot would be honored that wasn't beneficial to anyone. After arriving on time only to have no one home more than one occasion, it was time to move on. I ended up quitting my volunteer job, but not before I bought the little girl a Cinderella dress for Christmas, something she would otherwise never have received.

I didn't let that incident sway me from the belief in the benefits of Volunteering. It not only gets us out of ourselves by doing something for others, but also gives us a feeling of accomplishment. I did find another volunteer job, which was working in the kitchen at the OASIS Senior Center during lunchtime. It was a way to give something back to the facility for their generosity and support toward our grandparent group. My lifelong volunteer job, however will always be my commitment to help other grandparents who are experiencing visitation issues.

CONSULTING WITH AN ATTORNEY: can provide grandparents with a legal perspective that will help them better understand their options. So many grandparents are under the impression that if there is a grandparent rights law they will automatically get visitation. I went to court and even though I had standing, the judge didn't provide a court ordered visitation order and the second time I went to court to use my new law, the judge denied my civil rights to be heard.

Sometimes grandparents are successful in achieving court ordered visitation, which is completely under the judge's control—something everyone should understand before filing a petition. But a consultation is always a good idea in order to receive some clarification and help grandparents make a decision about taking the legal route.

GOING UNDERCOVER: is not for everyone. Grandparents who have communicated that it would be more painful for them to see the child and not be able to touch or talk to them than not see them at all have settled on less intense versions.

Some grandparents have hired private investigators to locate the child as a result of the parents moving away without providing a forwarding address, which is about as far it goes. Knowing where they are is sometimes comfort enough.

Some grandparents take it a step farther by parking near the child's school and hoping for a quick glimpse as they leave campus. It's also not uncommon to do a drive by past their houses. Facebook and Instagram have become valuable resources for grandparents by providing a window into the lives of grandchildren that they otherwise wouldn't have.

During the years that I've been working with disenfranchised grandparents, I know of only one other grandparent who did some surveillance. Again, this is something that is not widely broadcast, especially when the child is young, so there could be others like me who pushed the limits.

What grandparents may want to consider is, once a grandchild turns eighteen, they most likely are not going to come knocking on your door. Case after case, I have seen this happen. It's up to the grandparents to locate the now adult grandchild. Another good reason for keeping tabs on them whether or not you go the surreptitious route; at least you can be ready to take action when they hit eighteen without wasting anymore valuable time trying to locate them.

Would I do it again? Absolutely. I can't imagine going from age five or eight until the age of 18 to see a grandchild.

I will always have a chronicle of his childhood, no matter how limited.

I had the opportunity to watch him grow up by making sure that I saw him each and every year.

And most important, he knows.

Made in the USA
San Bernardino, CA
07 July 2020

74571044R00088